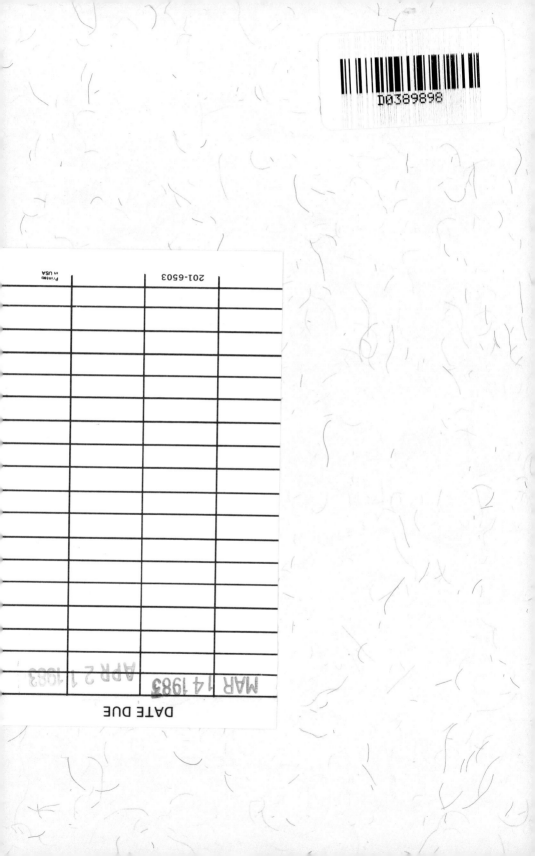

Trusteeship and the
Management of Foundations

Donald R. Young
Rockefeller University

and

Wilbert E. Moore
Russell Sage Foundation

RUSSELL SAGE FOUNDATION
New York — 1969

PUBLICATIONS OF RUSSELL SAGE FOUNDATION

Russell Sage Foundation was established in 1907 by Mrs. Russell Sage for the improvement of social and living conditions in the United States. In carrying out its purpose the Foundation conducts research under the direction of members of the staff or in close collaboration with other institutions, and supports programs designed to improve the utilization of social science knowledge. As an integral part of its operations, the Foundation from time to time publishes books or pamphlets resulting from these activities. Publication under the imprint of the Foundation does not necessarily imply agreement by the Foundation, its Trustees, or its staff with the interpretations or conclusions of the authors.

© 1969

RUSSELL SAGE FOUNDATION

Printed in the United States of America
Library of Congress Catalog Card Number: 75–87819

Preface

THE FEAR OF IRRESPONSIBLE POWER AT THE COMMAND OF occupants of positions of influence over the lives of others keeps appearing in the rhetoric of social critics in democratic societies. Yet over the years, we have noted in our thinking about the problem of widespread and decentralized decisional authorities in a pluralistic social order that the key term "irresponsible" is difficult to pin down, unless one takes the rather irresponsible (because false) view that only a centralized political authority overseeing all significant social acts assures accountability of these acts. As sociologists we were long schooled to look for rules and their sanctions in all continuing and moderately orderly social relations, and even to find "private polities" and their appropriate legal systems in business corporations, universities, and other bureaucratically organized collectivities.

These rather general ideas, which seemed to us to cut through the empty dogma of some social criticism, found a focus on the rules and practices of the trusteeship of private philanthropic funds. The essays here presented are designed to bring into sharp focus the evolution of the rules, evolved in both law and custom, that guide those responsible for wise management of other people's money, and the way that general principles work out in the continuing (and mostly responsible) behavior of trustees. Our central interest is in the trustees of foundations with funds held "perpetually" for philanthropic purposes. This interest clearly reflects our common, though not overlapping, association with a foundation that is relatively old (and relatively modest) by American standards. Yet we found lessons in the norms and practices of foundation trusteeship that have wider application, and, indeed, illustrate the ways in which authority not supervised by an external center of control may be truly responsible, but may also fail to fulfill the confidence placed in that way of managing scarce resources. We seek to explore honorable con-

iii

duct and conscientious inadvertence as well as willful misuse of trust.

We present here a pair of essays, prepared in close cooperation in initial and detailed outlines, written independently, and mutually criticized in a way that only old friends and respected colleagues would tolerate. Both our intellectual preoccupations and our experiences with the circumstances of trusteeship led us to write separate but coordinate essays rather than attempting to meld our rather different perspectives and expositional styles into a fictitiously combined product. We think that, in addition to the glue on the back binding, this book is held together by common themes. The conscientious reader of a combined exposition would have detected differences in subject-matter and approach; we have made his task simpler by distinguishing the source of those differences.

The term "essays" has been used, here and again, advisedly. These contributions to a scant literature are not presented as research reports. The elementary facts about trustees are not in dispute, and scarcely need new confirmation. Rules, policies, and practices are less well authenticated, and to those we have turned our attention, each in his own way.

Aside from keen critical comment exchanged by the two authors in an enterprise that has reconfirmed their joy in an enduring friendship, we have had the benefit of comments by several knowledgeable critics. Dr. F. Emerson Andrews, president emeritus of The Foundation Center and a long-time student of American philanthropy at Russell Sage Foundation and at The Foundation Center, reviewed both essays in detail. Comments were also provided by Dr. Manning Pattillo, Dr. Andrews' successor at The Foundation Center. Helpful critical amendments, particularly on the law of trusts, were given by Dean Robert B. Yegge of the University of Denver College of Law and by Marion Fremont-Smith, of the Boston law firm of Choate, Hall & Stewart and a part-time staff member of Russell Sage Foundation.

The author of the first essay, Wilbert Moore, wishes to record and underscore his warm gratitude to the late Ian Weinberg, former student and close friend, who died in March, 1969, at a tragically early age. Professor Weinberg had an interest largely coincident with Moore's in the subject of trusteeship, and particularly in its historical evolution and sociological interpretation. Weinberg, indeed, took the time and trouble to suggest a very extensive revision of an intermediate draft of Moore's essay. Although Moore has mainly persisted in his original organization and language, he has, with Weinberg's explicit consent, included some of his material. Such borrowed ideas and information will, of course, be suitably noted in the text. Weinberg and Moore had hoped to undertake a joint exploration of the significance of trust in human affairs generally. Although some hope remained until nearly the end of Weinberg's life, he died while this book was in proof. In recognition of debt and not its payment, Moore is dedicating his essay to the memory of Ian Weinberg: A good man, and true.

Both of the authors are understandably grateful that we have a common commitment to Russell Sage Foundation's continuing interest in studies of philanthropy, and therefore that the Foundation made possible this joint enterprise.

Common decency and immemorial custom require us to absolve our critics and to accept sole responsibility for the words set next to our names. We should be more fearful of that burden if the critics had not endeavored to save us from unspeakable transgressions. And, lest a note of coolness be inferred from our editorial separation, we publicly record our mutual gratitude and enduring relation as trusted colleagues and warm friends.

Donald R. Young
Wilbert E. Moore

Macungie, Pennsylvania
Princeton, New Jersey

Contents

vii

Trusteeship: A Combination of Institutional Principles

Wilbert E. Moore

Trusteeship: A Combination of Institutional Principles

Wilbert E. Moore[*]

TRUST IS AN ESSENTIAL INGREDIENT OF ENDURING HUMAN RELA-
tions. In its simplest and most general form it consists in a more
or less realistic confidence in fulfilled expectations: that persons
will behave according to the appropriate rules governing organizations and relations, that roles will be properly played, that
responsibilities will be met.

Trust, then, commonly involves mutuality of expectations,
and often reciprocity in services. Among friends, reciprocity of
expectations may be very general, any given claim on a trusted
relationship requiring no precisely counterbalancing claim but
only the assurance that, should need arise, an appropriate request would be honored. Trust often applies even when calcu-
lated self-interest is assumed, as in oral contracts. And the reciprocity need not be immediate, as in lending money or extending
credit for purchases. Violation of trust, of presumably shared ex-

* The author wishes to dedicate this essay to the memory of Ian Weinberg:
former student, warm friend, and despite these disadvantages, brilliant
sociologist. We are all poorer when an old and wise man dies; we are
immeasurably poorer when a young and wise man dies.

pectations, is uniformly disruptive in social relations. It is met with sanctions ranging from mere severance and avoidance to more serious reprisals.

All fiduciary relations involve trust, but many of these, too, involve reciprocity. The investor in a corporation expects the members of company management to act in his interests to the best of their ability. The client of a professional places his trust in the professional's competence and conscientious performance in the client's interests.

These familiar examples involve normative principles that are by no means trivial. Our central interest in this essay, however, is in a highly developed form of fulfillment of trust, but without reciprocity. The trustee of a charitable trust, such as a foundation or other endowment, is expected to act honorably, fulfilling the expectations of a donor perhaps long deceased and those of his colleagues, on behalf of beneficiaries, but with no *quid pro quo*. It might be said to be an almost unrequited or asymmetrical fulfillment of trust.

The type of trusteeship with which we are primarily concerned here involves the supervision or management of resources destined for charitable uses. In the typical case the trustees of a fund or an organization constitute an organized collectivity, with discretionary powers in such matters as allocation of resources and choice of salaried staff to advise trustees or to carry out the prescribed activities. Again, in the typical case the resources supervised constitute an endowment with a long life or "in perpetuity" from one or more original donors, with varying degrees of discretion in the time limits and on the uses to which the resources may be put, including classes of possible recipients of expendable funds. Prime examples of trusteeship as examined here are provided by the independent foundations having little or no remaining influence by the original donor or his close associates. Yet most of the principles of trusteeship are little affected if the donor is alive and has a voice in supervising the trust, if the resources are to be liquidated, or if the source of funds is from current gifts rather than a past gift or legacy. Trustees of private colleges and universities commonly supervise resources that represent physical assets from prior donors, income-yielding general and special endowments, grants and contracts for research activities, students' fees, sale of admissions to athletic events, and so on. These various sources make a difference in detail, particularly with respect to the trustees' discretion in their use, but may have little effect on the formal responsibilities of trusteeship.

Note, however, that with respect to certain funds such as gate receipts, the responsibility of "trustees" is not strictly a fiduciary one, but rather contractual. In early 1969 some Columbia University students, in an unprecedented legal action, petitioned the New York State Supreme Court—a court of first jurisdiction in that state—to dismiss the University's trustees for violation of contract. The students did not allege any misuse of trust funds, for on such a complaint they would have no cause of action, but rather that the trustees had failed to fulfill explicit or implicit contractual obligations to provide a suitable faculty and a suitable environment for higher education.[1] Since students in private universities are partly beneficiaries of charitable endowments and other gifts and, in most instances, partly contributors to the costs of their education, their relations with university authorities is complex or at least mixed.

The responsibilities of trustees of resources destined for charitable or philanthropic purposes are symbolized in some of the most value-laden terms in the language. The trustee owes the duty of *prudence* in the management of resources, for he is, after all, not handling his own assets; if he were, and acted imprudently, he might expect some high risk of loss or punishment by the impersonal forces of financial or other markets. He is not permitted such discretion on behalf of others.

The trustee also owes the duty of *loyalty*, to the general purposes established by donors, to the welfare of intended beneficiaries, and, commonly, to the ongoing organization or collectivity for which he has assumed some responsibility.

The loyalty expected of the trustee is especially interesting, for, we have noted, it is an extension of a principle that normally applies to such relationships as those obtaining between a professional practitioner and his client, or the manager of a private

---

[1] See Murray Schumach, "12 at Columbia Sue to Oust Trustees," *New York Times*, January 11, 1969, pp. 1, 16.

trust, in the interests of named beneficiaries. The trustees with whom we are concerned owe a loyalty to the interests of un-named beneficiaries, though the range of possible claimants may be narrow or wide. Indeed, the norm for trustees' actions is that they will be *disinterested*: that is, not in the first instance deter-mined by the self-interest of the trustees and, if necessary, even contrary to such self-interest.

To refer to such criteria of conduct as formal responsibilities does not necessarily imply that they are entirely and adequately codified in public law and enforced by executive agencies of the state. Much of the honorable conduct of trustees (and, of course, some dishonorable conduct) remains outside the public purview, being sanctioned by common usage and the expectations of "sig-nificant others." What legal supervision is available, particularly in the United States, appears more as an afterthought, a by-product of the concession of tax exemption, than as a forthright exercise of public concern over the management of private ac-tions with an avowedly public purpose.

The title of this essay refers to a combination of institutional principles, and that is the view of trusteeship that will be pur-sued here. The most inclusive principle is that of fiduciary ac-tions and responsibilities, which applies to trustees of charitable endowments, but also to the management of public wealth and current accounts and the savings and investments of private citi-zens in the form of life insurance, bank accounts, and partici-pating shares of stock in private corporations. The principle of lay control of organizations that may be manned by professional or quasi-professional operating staffs for carrying out the organi-zation's several missions is very extensive in American society, and by no means limited to the custody of endowments. The legal accountabilities of trustees derive from a complex body of Anglo-American law, but those rules comprise only a part of the law of trusts. Thus trusteeship as we shall examine it further represents not a total amalgamation of these institutional principles, but rather their intersection. The strategy of this exploration of trus-teeship is to proceed from the most general principle, that of fiduciary relations, to the principle of lay control, and thence to the law of trusts, the final destination being the particular body of rules and administrative arrangements that influence but do not precisely determine the actions of foundation trustees. None of these bodies of principles is singular and unequivocal, and even their combination leaves discretionary latitude to the actors in various small and large dramas. The exercise of discretion is explored here in terms of the institutional order, and by Donald R. Young in the following essay in pragmatic terms of trustee decision-making.

The Fiduciary Principle

The first normative principle, or set of norms, that helps to define the institutional setting of contemporary trusteeship is the broadest of all. It is that certain individuals assume responsibility for the welfare of others. By extension, the principle requires that this other-regarding responsibility be fulfilled even at the possible expense of the self-interest of the person assuming such burdens. We shall call this the fiduciary principle, for that concept rather precisely encompasses the notion that many interests are entrusted to the management of others, whose position requires that they fulfill such obligations faithfully.

The principle is thus broader than the law of trusts, which concerns the disposition of private resources on behalf of beneficiaries who may not be able to manage those resources for themselves, and in any event are not permitted to do so by the trust arrangement. The principle is also somewhat broader than the set of norms relating to lay control, but it is more closely proximate to that principle, for it admits responsible amateurism; but fiduciary relations may also be technical and thus more closely approximate the notion that trustees should be persons of *unusual* probity and prudence, discharging responsibility for the less fortunate in ability or station in life in return for their standing in the community.

There may have been a time, now overfondly recalled through the usual distortions of nostalgia, when free-born citizens of the Western world disposed of most of their economic resources at their own discretion. There is little need for fiduciary management if private property consists mainly of land and other tangible goods, and public property is poorly distinguishable from the private property of hereditary monarchs or a safely land-based

aristocracy. Private holders of usable resources might well act
responsibly toward those to whom they acknowledge particular
relations—for example, wives and children—but not for impersonal or anonymous others. (We shall note later that parenthood
is the primordial form of trusteeship, that fiduciary relations toward *known* beneficiaries are ancient and persistent forms of
social responsibility.)

Fiduciary Relations in the Economy.   Although no exact metric
appears available for measuring the degree of structural change
in the management of resources, it is scarcely debatable that in
modern (and therefore complex and interdependent) economies,
human resources are increasingly managed in a fiduciary way.
It would be too glib and misleading to say that we are busily re-
instituting feudalism, the central principle of which was an
orderly network and hierarchy of fiduciary relations. Yet some
modern fiduciary patterns more nearly resemble feudal arrangements than they do a completely individualistic economic order.

This "abdication" of individual responsibility for tending to
his own economic affairs is most conspicuous precisely in the
"private" sector of societies that admit and foster private investments and transactions. One may still find individuals with discretionary financial resources who decide for themselves how
those will be used: for example, in buying real estate, art objects,
or other physical manifestations of wealth. Generally, however,
individual (or family) economic resources are represented in
bank deposits, life insurance and annuities, public or corporate
bonds, or equity shares in "private" corporations and investment
trusts. In effect, these investments are managed in a fiduciary
capacity by the presumably responsible officials of manufacturing
and financial organizations.

These arrangements are so widespread that they touch a very
large part of the population. It is not only (and perhaps not primarily) persons of great affluence that have given over the management of some part of their well-being to others. The bank
depositor, the investor having a few shares of stock, the purchaser of life insurance, the prospective beneficiary of a private
pension plan—all these have placed their trust in the managers
of funds in a fiduciary capacity.

In Western "capitalist" countries, which afford most of these investment opportunities to the individual or private collectivity (such as a labor union or professional association), a convenient and conventional fiction is maintained. That fiction is that investors are in fact represented by business managers, the weight of influence being proportionate to the amount invested. The fiduciary principle is thus a quasi-democratic one: those who control the resources of others do so in behalf of the proper clients, and are held accountable through processes of voting shares of stock (or their equivalent). In effect, however, depositors, purchasers, and investors turn out to be even less effectual than a political electorate.[2]

The essence of the problem with private, but impersonal, fiduciary relations is that the comfortable assumption is made that the actions of responsible officials in furthering their own interests will redound to the interests of other nominally represented but usually quiescent parties. This assumption is, at best, only approximately true. Few business managers, or members of corporate boards of directors, are likely to enjoy unusual prosperity while overseeing a losing enterprise—though that can happen. But when the enterprise prospers, the decision as to how the gains will be divided is entrusted to those same managers. Of the various interests to which corporate managers must be attentive (suppliers, customers, public law enforcement agencies and tax collectors, creditors, stockholders) those of the managers themselves are given very high priority.[3]

The investor, of course, is not without recourse. He can try to line up other dissidents and throw the rascals out through a "proxy fight." That is very expensive business, and he had better have backing from a major investor before trying it. He can, alternatively, simply sell his shares (the usual tactic of a dissatisfied stockholder), hoping to find a more honorable management elsewhere. He can, as a further course of action, simply sit still, in possibly grumbling quiescence, if his interest is in capital

---

[2] See John Kenneth Galbraith, *The New Industrial State* (Boston: Houghton Mifflin Co., 1967), especially pp. 72–85.

[3] See Wilbert E. Moore, *The Conduct of the Corporation* (New York: Random House, 1962).

gains at market prices for his shares, and he regards the amount of current dividends as a trivial consideration. He can, finally, and with little hope, bring a stockholder's suit against the company for mismanagement of his investment. On the record, he may as well save his effort, for the courts in Britain or America seem loath to review the practices of corporate managers in their use of other people's money. The presumption runs strongly that "management knows best" in the fiduciary position. This is at times a conspicuously false presumption, but it certainly saves the courts from being burdened with tedious, technical, and often trivial litigation.

Not all investors, or beneficiaries of the efforts of others in their behalf, are in the same position as the equity stockholder in a private corporation. Owners of life insurance policies, whether in joint stock or mutual companies, have a form of investment. Collectively, the policy-owners of a mutual insurance company or a mutual savings back are owners of the company. Owners of policies in mutual insurance companies are, in almost all jurisdictions, permitted to receive dividends on their state-fixed premiums for insurance bought. Owners of savings accounts in mutual banks are less fortunate. Unlike the owners of a life insurance policy, they do not commonly have the right to vote on directors of the company. Moreover, the state banking commissioner (commonly guided by the Federal Reserve Board) sets the upper limit of interest to be paid on deposits. This means that a *good* bank management for a mutual bank has serious problems. That management must constantly dispose of new investment income, for it is prohibited from returning to the investors (depositors) the actual, rather than the administratively fixed return on investment. In sum, the depositors collectively *own* mutual savings banks, and have not even a nominal voice in their control or in the rate of return on their investments. The fiduciary principle is carried to a point that is, in a word, extreme.

By common law and statute the interests of potential beneficiaries of charitable foundations are under the purview of the attorney general of the appropriate jurisdiction, though, we shall see, this is in fact a very weak control. The protections against corporate mismanagement are even weaker, and rest with no designated public agency other than the courts, which are ineffective. We may yet see a commissioner of corporations to add a measure of official weight to a fiduciary position that is especially subject to possible abuse. The Securities and Exchange Commission, a federal agency still not wholly beloved by the wheeler-dealers in the market for stocks and other shares in dubious enterprises, does represent a measure of control over the marketing of equities. There is simply no effective control over the current management of corporations other than the control, infrequently exercised by holders of the corporation's obligations (stocks, bonds, bank notes, and the like), with or without recourse to administrative agencies and the courts.

Management of Public Resources. Fiduciary responsibilities are also assumed by public officials, whether elective or appointive. The management of public property and the disposition of public funds is supposed to be in the public interest: either all citizens without apparent discrimination, or special categories of citizens (for example, war veterans, homeless children, or others lacking adequate personal and private resources) according to some explicit standards of redistribution of assets.

Any exercise of political authority, short of naked terror, rests eventually on a nonrational assumption of legitimacy: the divine right of kings, the routinized charisma ("apostolic succession") of popes, the superior political wisdom of Communist Party commissars, or the authenticating of an electorate to which genuine choices have been presented. The principle of authority will affect the accountability of authorities. For rulers and office-holders who claim, and are at least tacitly accorded, rights of rule that are not subject to current and widespread explicit consent, there is a strong tendency to emphasize consistency with tradition and the preservation and enhancement of the position of the collectivity (the church, the national state) as such. At an extreme, a French ruler could assert with dubious propriety, *"l'état, c'est moi,"* but even such an absolutist principle of political legitimacy could scarcely evade some fiduciary responsibility for present subjects, as well as those now dead and those yet to live. If current accountabilities to lesser creatures turned out to be paternalistic, and, to a distressing degree, whimsical, they still existed.

The modern democratic, or quasi-democratic state affords not only the management of public assets, but also the redistribution of what might otherwise be private assets through taxation and various forms of welfare disbursements. Some services are afforded the citizen whether he likes them or not: police and fire protection, water supply and sewage disposal, compulsory education for children, national defense budgets, contributory pension plans, and a host of other public services for general or special constituencies.

The activities of "welfare states" (and all post-industrial societies deserve that designation) shift fiduciary responsibilities from private managers of other people's money to public ones, and the mechanisms of possible self-protection from the marketplace to the voting booth (if one is meaningfully available). In both instances a nominally independent judiciary may, on occasion, protect the interests of claimants against the errors and possibly venal and self-serving acts of those who are supposed to be acting on behalf of investors, citizens, taxpayers, or other relatively helpless aggregates of persons nominally represented by others. In Britain and in America the courts have generally mantled themselves with conservatism—under the rule of precedent, the common law doctrine of *stare decisis* (let the decision stand) —even while enterprising innovators and even legislators were radically changing the circumstances of social action. Nevertheless, attention to changing circumstances has, in these latter days, shown itself in the deliberations of courts of appellate jurisdiction, with the consequence that the meaning of accountability does get redefined from time to time.

Responsibility for Private Philanthropy. If the fiduciary principle had a dubious propriety in absolutist political regimes, gradually asserted through electoral and judicial reforms, and still has a somewhat delicate standing in private corporate affairs, it has an ancient and relatively honorable lineage in nonprofit and nonpolitical matters of moment.

We encounter substantial numbers of selected citizens who give both time and labor to affairs other than their own, under rather severe restrictions in their discretion, and in the full light of a collectivity of similarly selected individuals who may, nevertheless, have less than consensual views on any particular issue.

Let us, as a start, take the most cynical view of motivation of what is, normally, not directly rewarded activity. A small foundation has been established by a living donor, for some combination of reasons involving public service and tax avoidance, with a board of trustees comprising several members of the family, a trusted business associate or two, and the donor's attorney. If not directly recompensed, why should these individuals serve? For a variety of reasons, including hope of future benefits and fear of immediate withdrawal of patronage, most trustees may have little option.

Let us take as another, and not rare, example, the man of renowned if circumspect success, in a managerial or professional position, recommended by associates who are current trustees as a person of wisdom, judgment, and, possibly, knowledge in an area presently represented on the board of trustees thinly or not at all. The basis for inviting him to serve may be clearer than the basis for his acceptance. For the prospective exerciser of fiduciary responsibilities, it may be an accolade, a further confirmation of his hard-won arrival at high estate. We should not reject the possibility that he wishes to be of service.

What we encounter here is a certain sense of *noblesse oblige*, which may or may not bespeak a kind of uneasy conscience, and is not at all uniform among successful men. The call to serve suggests to the individual invited to participate in decisions affecting the welfare of the less-privileged that his exalted position gives him both the acumen and the duty of spending other people's money wisely.

The fiduciary principle appears in one of its purest forms among the trustees of foundations completely independent of original donors. The executives and directors of corporations or banks and mutual insurance companies receive material rewards, as do most elective and appointive public officials. The professional stands in a fiduciary relation to his client, but normally does not go unrewarded for the trust placed in his care and competence. The trustee of a private school or college is often an alumnus, and although the familial relations signified by references to *alma mater* may not be taken too seriously, there is a kind of institutional loyalty mixed with other incentives to serve. The typical trustee of an established foundation assumes responsibility for the welfare of an organization, and especially for its purposes and beneficiaries as a kind of philanthropic service, often untainted by other loyalties and obligations.

Any fiduciary position implies power, limited by responsibility. The modes of assuring responsibility, we have noted, are variable according to types of positions, and it is fair to say that they are not equally or uniformly effective. We shall see that the trustees of private foundations are among the least subject to effective formal controls, for most boards enjoy considerable discretionary authority, and, above all, have the virtually unchallengeable privilege of nonfeasance or inadequate performance. But boards are also collegial bodies, that is, collective bodies that have common responsibilities. Although there are social situations in which the outcome of action may be determined by the least moral participant, that cynical view is unlikely to apply to collectivities of persons who have assumed responsibility for the management of charitable funds. A better case could be made for the contrary assumption of unusual influence by those who exhibit the greatest dedication to honorable principles.

It is always proper to look for or speculate about cynical interpretations of social behavior, if for no other reason than to avoid being unduly naive. It is equally proper, however, to entertain the possibility of alternative or additional interpretations. Just as one cannot safely reject some degree of genuinely charitable motivation on the part of donors of funds, we cannot reject some interest in honorable and unrequited service on the part of the custodians of such funds.

Heirs to a long evolutionary development in Anglo-American law, a possibly equally long institutional principle of (select) lay control, and representing a fiduciary principle that is constantly more extensive and diversified in its manifestations, foundation trustees and closely comparable doers of good works exercise honorable responsibilities in private philanthropy. Their contributions of time and wisdom are generally without direct material reward and, indeed, are often unsung except among immediate colleagues. Only a minority achieve public acclaim for their duties, and those few are likely to be sufficiently well-placed occupationally and financially to indulge their interest as valuable and valued amateurs in private service for public causes. Others serve quietly, with varying degrees of conscientiousness and wisdom. They are, of course, not alone as volunteers in worthy causes,[4] but they do oversee the expenditure of sums that seem small only in comparison with the United States federal budget, and loom large in the life-view of countless researchers, welfare organizations, artists, and producers of culture, not elsewhere classified.

The Principle of Lay Control

Partly because of the complexity of the law of trusts, to which we shall attend later, lawyers appear with disproportionate frequency both as custodians of private trusts (for named beneficiaries) and as trustees of endowed organizations. Even in the investment trusts of "private" corporations, lawyers have played a prominent if not dominant part. Yet lawyers are not necessarily wise as substitute parents for children, to say nothing of having special knowledge of investments, manufacturing, education, hospital administration, or the support of various activities within the purposes of a foundation. Though professionals in the practice of law, they must commonly be regarded as laymen when serving as trustees.

This brings us to a second major institutional principle involved in trusteeship, the principle of lay control. Just as the legal rules affecting the powers and duties of trustees of philanthropic enterprises represent only part of the general principles of the law of trusts, the principle of lay control has wider application than that represented in trusteeship.

The historic origin of that rather curious organizational principle is obscure. It may well have originated in the ancient and continuing English practice of seeking royal or noble patronage for schools, hospitals, military units, and what not. In the English higher educational system, the office of chancellor is almost purely honorific, the actual chief executive being a vice-chancellor with properly academic credentials.

---

[4] See, for example, David L. Sills, *The Volunteers* (Glencoe, Ill.: Free Press, 1957). (Publisher now located in New York.)

The Layman as Cultivated Amateur. Yet to the degree that such positions are simply symbolic, we are not dealing with lay control. It might be argued, however, that such positions were not always solely honorific, and that many lay advisory and administrative committees and boards meanwhile have persisted in placing trust in the judgment of what might be called the "cultivated amateur." Weinberg, in fact, argues that charitable benefactions in the sixteenth to eighteenth centuries—when lay trusteeship became firmly established—came from prosperous merchants who could not enter the aristocracy, and avoided both the clergy and the aristocracy as supervisors of testamentary funds.[5] Note that in most instances the persons selected for service as trustees, school board members, or similar positions do *not* represent a cross-section of the community, but rather men of some standing or eminence. One should also recall that the principle of lay control was certainly established at a time when adults with an advanced education represented a very small segment of the adult population. In England, especially, the educated minority was likely to be drawn from the nobility, the merchants, the gentry, and the clergy. And very little of that education was technical in the sense of preparation for particular occupations, but rather classical and historical, and, in that sense, liberal. Such education was considered quite proper for public administration in the civil service as well as for elective office. A society that would entrust its government to cultivated amateurs would also draw upon the same limited constituency for other important duties, including the supervision of private trusts and endowments.

At least in English legal evolution, the "secularization of philanthropy," to be discussed subsequently, meant control of charitable benefactions by trustees drawn from the laity (rather than the clergy), chiefly from the same successful mercantile groups that produced most of the bequests. Lay control thus meant freedom from *clerical* control, and supervision of the probity of

---

[5] Ian Weinberg, personal communication, June 11, 1968. This accords with conclusions of Jordan. See W. K. Jordan, *Philanthropy in England, 1480–1660* (New York: Russell Sage Foundation, 1959), especially p. 247. Jordan attributes to donors . . . "a disposition to vest their endowments securely in trustworthy lay hands. . . ."

trustees passed, with the Reformation, from the ecclesiastical courts to courts in Chancery (proceedings in equity rather than in law, narrowly defined).

> It was then [at the Reformation] that charity in England became an independent institution, with trusteeship as its juridical basis. Instead of making a direct or conditional gift to a religious body the property was given in trust; the donation is administered as a separate patrimony; the trustee is a person trusted by the donor; beneficiaries are all those who fall within the purpose of the gift.[6]

We should note, in passing, that the position of attorneys as trustees is ambiguous with respect to the principle of lay control, for it might be assumed that their technical skills are called upon in matters relating to the limits of discretionary action. Most commonly, however, in well-established organizations such questions are likely to arise rarely, and when they do, it is common practice to rely upon "outside" legal counsel. The disproportionate representation of attorneys among foundation and similar trustees probably arises from a combination of circumstances: (1) Of the "leading" members of the community from which trustees are selected, lawyers share with clergymen a long tradition of public service. (2) For established lawyers, such as senior partners in highly respected firms, maintenance of reputation and income has a very slight if any correlation with the length of the work week spent at strictly technical tasks. (This availability of discretionary time is also true of some clergymen and some university professors.) (3) Somewhat more than incidentally, lawyers are likely to have been involved in establishing foundations. Particularly in the smaller family foundation one or more attorneys are likely to be among the donor's trusted advisers, and when this circumstance is coupled with the ambiguity noted above, their selection is understandable.

The principle of lay control, indeed, penetrates into the heart of the legal and judicial system. Jury trials represent an assertion of the wisdom of the laity, though contesting litigants have

---

[6] Christian de Wolf, *The Trust and Corresponding Institutions in the Civil Law* (Brussels: Bruylont, 1965), p. 147. I owe this reference, and the general point to which it refers, to Ian Weinberg's suggested revision of this essay, noted in our Preface.

been represented by "learned" counselors, and the proceedings presided over by a "learned" judge. The importance of this judicial procedure was underscored in the early nineteenth century by no less an observer than Alexis de Tocqueville.[7]

Selection of Suitable Laymen.   The laymen chosen to supervise matters of some public concern are by no means a random sample of adults. In addition to lawyers, bankers and corporate executives are commonly overrepresented. Yet methods of selection differ substantially among various types of organizations. The regents of state universities are commonly named by the governor, though often terms of appointment are staggered so that no governor in a single term can "control" the entire board. Public school boards are commonly elected in the United States, independently of party affiliation and in separate elections (which usually entice a small minority of the qualified electorate into voting). Some organizations substantially dependent on current contributions make contributors the electorate for selecting trustees. At least one foundation with a substantial principal fund assigns voting rights in foundation decisions proportionate to amounts given to the foundation by the donor and his descendants, in units of $1000 per vote.[8]

Private schools and colleges often permit alumni to elect some or all of the trustees, from among their own number, though other, nonalumni trustees may be selected by the board. Some organizations have charters in which the occupants of particular positions—a mayor, a chief judge of a judicial district—name some or all of the governing board. The community foundation generally follows this pattern, but with some further significant features with respect to the functions of trusteeship. Following the precedent set by the first such foundation—the Cleveland Foundation established in 1914—a distinction is drawn between the trustee in the narrow and technical sense, and the distribution committee. Trusteeship is almost uniformly lodged in one

---

[7] See Alexis de Tocqueville, *Democracy in America*, edited by J. P. Mayer and Max Lerner (New York: Harper & Row, 1966), p. 249.

[8] "Amended Certificate of Incorporation of the Richardson Foundation, Inc.," typescript copy on file at The Foundation Center, New York.

or more banks. The trustee is concerned with the investment management of funds, which are the pooled resources from a variety of donors. The distribution committee is responsible for the allocation of income to charitable causes, and it is the distribution committee that is typically selected by various other boards or individual office-holders acting *ex officio*.[9] Thus the discretionary powers and responsibilities normally held by foundation and other trustees is subdivided in the governance of community foundations. The division is not necessarily sharp, however, since the trustee (the board of directors of a named bank) may be among the selectors of the distribution committee.[10]

The board of trustees of nearly all other endowed foundations is self-perpetuating, that is *cooptive*. (In effect, this is also true of the boards of directors of corporations with widely dispersed equity ownership. Short of a genuine proxy fight, commonly a consequence of the attempt of another corporation or closely linked small group of persons to secure a sufficient—though minority—position to control the naming of a board and therefore to choose salaried executives, the nominal electorate for corporate directors is even more apathetic than the electorate for public offices.)

The cooptive principle means that current trustees choose their own successors. Although the election is collective, a kind of informal code could develop by which a retiring trustee is permitted to name his own successor, subject only to routine ratification by his peers. In any event, a relatively homogeneous group of trustees will generally select new members at least of their own social status, if not better. Against the presumptive advantages of continuity of policies and point of view and of capacity to identify the important intellectual and moral qualities demanded, one must set the potential disadvantages of stuffy conservatism in the face of changing situations.

---

[9] See F. Emerson Andrews, *Philanthropic Foundations* (New York: Russell Sage Foundation, 1956), pp. 32–34, 65–66.

[10] See *Ibid.*, Appendix E, for the charter of the Mount Vernon (Ohio) Community Trust. In this instance two banks serve as trustees, and their boards of directors select two of the five members of the distribution committee.

We thus reach a paradox that needs to be explicated and explored. The paradox is that the principle of lay control should keep professional staffs and salaried administrators responsive to the diverse and changing character of constituents, potential beneficiaries, and other public interests served by a philanthropic organization. Yet the pragmatic situation is that the salaried administrative or professional staffs for whom the trustees hold themselves accountable are, in the nature of the case, more likely to know about, and to be attentive to, change than are the part-time amateurs who are the trustees. A self-perpetuating board may well achieve a kind of self-satisfied insularity that almost defies attention to fundamental change in the conditions appropriate for sensible policy.

Unless there is a rather extensive and often informal exchange of information and opinion between salaried officers (university administrators and professors, hospital chiefs, foundation staffs) and trustees, there may well develop a situation in which the laymen seem to be superseding the views of the active practitioners, and the practitioners feel it necessary to line up with the intended beneficiaries against the trustees. Beneficiaries have no legal and little practical access to trustees, but salaried staffs may become their spokesmen.

The deeper-lying paradox is really a simple restatement of the last few paragraphs. The idea of achieving responsibility to public interest through lay control by conscientious trustees has several inherent limitations. (1) Whatever the mode of selection of trustees, there is no certain way to ensure that current trustees are either generally competent or specifically attentive to changing circumstances of operation. (2) Since current trustees are more likely to be representative of their peers and predecessors than of relevant staffs, clients, and constituencies, the principle of lay control may be effectively subverted by the relative immunity of trustees to current accountability as long as broad discretionary limits are not transgressed. (3) The paradox deepens by viewing alternatives. Election of trustees by recognized constituencies (which, like the urban Negro poor, may not recognize themselves as meaningful constituencies), or having guardians named by an elective political official, may aggravate potential difficulties rather than resolving them. There is no reason to suppose that choices made by the uninformed will be superior to those made by custodians who are at least informed by the past if not anticipating the future.

Lay Trustees and Professional Staffs. The system that provides accountability to a lay board for the actions of professional, or at least salaried, officers of organizations is another example of the principle of checks and balances. It would be both surprising and disturbing if quiet consensus uniformly prevailed, for that would deny the basis for having potentially divergent interests weighed in. What is suggested here is that the professional staffs of universities or foundations owe a duty to participate in the "socializing" of new trustees, partly to complement and partly to offset the do's and don'ts they will receive from their fellow overseers.

Boards of trustees are commonly comprised of individuals who are professional, or at least exceptionally successful, each in his own occupation or field of endeavor.[11] Yet the trustees commonly remain laymen in the area of primary interest represented by a school, a church, a charity, a foundation. The nuances of the relations between "professional" staffs and highly selected and therefore unrepresentative lay trustees are highly instructive, though difficult to typify, and even more difficult to quantify.

We can draw some extreme examples or types from extant knowledge, but we should not be so bold as to assign frequency distributions to the types.

One type of trustee-staff relationship is represented by the situation in which a highly competent (perhaps, in his own field, a professional) trustee is hoodwinked into going along with an essentially silly proposal by salaried professionals, on the ground that the professionals must know what they are about. (The extreme example is the school board member or uni-

---

[11] We did not undertake a new survey of the occupational composition of foundation or other boards of trustees. Casual examination of trustees identified in Marianna O. Lewis, editor, *The Foundation Directory, Edition 3* (New York: published for The Foundation Library Center by Russell Sage Foundation, 1967) reveals the expected predominance of lawyers and business executives. For an earlier survey, see F. Emerson Andrews, *Philanthropic Foundations,* previously cited, pp. 63–91.

versity trustee, who in dealing with educational matters, is given
the false assurance of doctrine by professional spokesmen.)

An opposite extreme can be readily found: the lay trustee
pretending, perhaps because of his protected position, to be an
expert on matters about which he is profoundly ignorant. This
situation may display itself in many forms:

Item: A prominent lawyer as trustee assumes that since law
is a ubiquitous aspect of social relations, he correctly understands social relations.

Item: A father of several children, all well-behaved and ap-
propriately striving after goals consistent with parental aspira-
tions, assumes that he understands the cross-section of public
school children. He runs a successful campaign for the school
board.

Item: A college trustee, named in the hope that his wealth
from a self-made successful business may in part come to his
college, would like the curriculum to be more practical, and
especially to emphasize subjects appropriate to a business career.

Item: A trustee, successful in his occupation, has become a
fairly knowledgeable amateur, an *aficionado,* of a subject represented by a member of the professional staff. He professes to lack
confidence in the professional staff member, for reasons ranging
from childish petulance for not having been given suitable defer-
ence or welcomed into the limited confraternity of the profession, to a seemingly superior show of technical judgment.

Some morals follow from these only faintly hypothetical examples of trustee-staff relations. The first moral is that the definition of trustee powers and responsibilities cannot end with
legal responsibilities. Those responsibilities are notably broad,
and therefore notably imprecise. In technical effect, trustees *own*
and administer resources for various purposes of public welfare. Yet the trustees are bound in by legal and conventional
rules of conduct, for they are obliged to use those resources for
broad or stipulated public purposes, but almost never for their
own.

The second moral is that the relations among various centers
of poorly specified powers and responsibilities is bound to produce tensions. Any social system that would make technical experts accountable to lay supervision in their technical activities

has to have an underlying suspicion of technicians. Yet any social system that would grant broad privileges and immunities to its technicians before any hint of external control sets in has to have a kind of confidence in people who know things.

We began this portion of the essay with an inquiry into the principle of lay control, and we have necessarily come full circle to the question—who's in charge here? The principle of professionalism is so strong that one might guess that it would emerge in triumph. Yet there was invented, a few centuries ago and no doubt for rather different reasons, a system of lay supervision of what might otherwise be considered purely professional concerns. That principle persists, and has a basis in law and lore that is partially represented by the law of trusteeship, though that law is scarcely singular and certainly not without unresolved ambiguities.

Legal Evolution of Trusteeship

The notion that some members of society may have rights, or deserve concern, without effective means for assuring their proper interests is not a modern invention. Indeed, throughout the human species infants are unable to sustain life unaided, and were they not cared for by others (by biological parents in the vast majority of cases), the species itself would cease to exist. Persons who take, or have thrust upon them, the nurturing of the young thus may be viewed as the primordial type of the trustee. (Whether parents or their substitutes have absolute discretion over the lives and fortunes of their helpless charges is an issue that has been resolved in many ways. Its exploration here would take us too far afield. Suffice it to say that in most "primitive" societies children represent, among other things, a future investment as compensation for current care, and in highly modernized societies, public interest in the young can supersede private control when necessary.)

Various civilizations, ancient or modern, have also recognized formal obligations for persons other than infants who are thought to deserve protection or assistance not directly available to them. Since morally endowed custom widely supported is not readily distinguishable from law in the proper sense of rules impersonally applied, it is scarcely worthwhile debating whether the care of the weak by the strong is an ancient and widespread legal principle. Laws and customs have varied, and except for the care of the young, variation is more evident than uniformity.

It seems more useful to sketch the direct legal antecedents of contemporary trusteeship. Two types of development in English law are of particular interest. The one may be called the *secularization of philanthropy,* and the other the *depersonalization of trusteeship.* We may well agree with Henry Allen Moe that "religion is the mother of philanthropy."[12] Certainly charity on behalf of the poor and otherwise disadvantaged was a prominent element in Judæo-Christian teaching, and not unknown in the Græco-Roman civilization with which it became combined. And certainly also in the predominantly Christian traditions of the Western world, the church was viewed for hundreds of years not only as itself a worthy direct recipient of gifts for holy purposes (not to mention guilt-assuaging payments for essentially private if other-worldly purposes, such as saying masses for the deceased donor), but also as an agency for redistribution on the behalf of the deserving needy.

Secularization of Philanthropy.   With the Reformation in England, the supervision of charitable bequests passed from the clerical courts to the Chancellor and the Chancery courts under his supervision. This meant, somewhat more than incidentally, that actions "in equity" were freed from the feudal principles still strongly prevalent in the "common" law courts. Thus property, and that especially meant land, could be "alienated" (bought and sold on the market). This transfer of responsibility also signalized what we have called the secularization of philanthropy. For, as Jordan notes,[13] extensive *private* endowments came to be supervised by lay (and in that sense secular) trustees. Yet the primary political purpose of this change was the assertion of the supremacy of the crown over the church. And that,

---

[12] Henry Allen Moe, "Notes on the Origin of Philanthropy in Christendom," *Proceedings of the American Philosophical Society*, vol. 105, April 21, 1961.

[13] W. K. Jordan, previously cited, pp. 126–142, 240–250.

in turn, signified an assertion of *public* interest in what we should now call welfare.[14] It follows that one should be cautious in viewing the "welfare state" as a strictly modern invention. Rather, it would appear that what is exceptional, certainly as among various modern countries, and also historically in the Anglo-American legal system, is the appearance of philanthropy that is both public and private and, above all, secular. Such philanthropy is public in the sense that its goals are consistent with widely held values, but private in its management and control of resources. Such philanthropy may also be religious in the very formal and technical sense of being subservient to unquestioned values, and even in the motivational sense of being prompted by explicitly religious motivations. Lines of distinction between underlying motivation and organized sponsorship may not be sharp. Yet it has been common for several centuries to draw a difference, if not an exact distinction, between "humanitarian" purposes and purposes specific to a particular religious organization. Philanthropy refers to "love of man," and not exclusively Presbyterian or Roman Catholic man, and if philanthropy has not distributed benefits with a perfectly equal, or even equitable, hand, part of the benefits certainly have been distributed without examining into the religious affiliation of beneficiaries or successful supplicants for foundation grants. Indeed, at least part of philanthropy has been secular concerning organized religion but also secular concerning organized polities; for the rights and privileges of citizens may be broader than the proper concerns of religious groups, but still narrower than (or at least different from) the claims of persons who appeal to values that cut across such identifications, such as scientific researchers, wherever located, or the poor, everywhere.

The secularization of philanthropy took place over a long period, and is and probably will remain partial. Aside from works of welfare supported by taxes collected by a secular state, a considerable portion of private charitable funds go to, and some of them through, religious bodies.[15] What is of immediate moment

---

[14] I owe this interpretation to Ian Weinberg from the unpublished essay noted in the Preface to this volume.

[15] See F. Emerson Andrews, *Philanthropic Giving* (New York: Russell Sage Foundation, 1950), pp. 73, 172–187.

is that portion of private philanthropy that is independent of constituted religious orders.

Depersonalization of Trusteeship. It is in the management of private philanthropy (and especially philanthropic endowments) that the "depersonalization of trusteeship" assumes significance.

From perhaps as early as the thirteenth century testamentary rights were clearly established,[16] with wills coming under the supervision of ecclesiastical courts. After the Reformation, the same powers were taken over by the royal courts, but specifically by the Chancery courts, not those of the "common law," which were exceptionally bound by customary (and therefore usually feudal) law. Moe[17] argues that the famous Elizabethan statutes on charitable trusts recognized a development that had been going on for some time: he traces it to William Langland's "The Vision of Piers the Plowman" of the fourteenth century. That development was a change of emphasis from strictly pious uses (masses for the dead, tapers for altars) to works of public welfare.

What were subsequently to be regarded as ends worthy of charitable gifts or bequests were laid out in the famous Elizabethan Statute of Charitable Uses.[18]

The preamble to the Statute noted that sovereigns and other well-disposed persons were making bequests, and gave examples:

> . . . some for releife of aged impotent and poore people, some for maintenance of sicke and maymed souldiers and marriners, schooles of learninge, free schooles and schollers in universities, some for repaire of bridges portes havens causewaies churches seabankes and highwaies, some for education and preferments of orphans, some for or towardes reliefe stocke or maintenance for howses of correction, some for mariages of poore maides, some for supportacion ayde and helpe of younge tradesmen, handiecraftesmen and persons decayed, and others for releife

---

[16] See Henry Allen Moe, "Notes on the Origin of Philanthropy in Christendom," previously cited.

[17] Henry Allen Moe, "The Vision of Piers the Plowman and the Law of Foundations," *Proceedings of the American Philosophical Society*, vol. 102, August 27, 1958, pp. 371–375.

[18] My source is W. K. Jordan, previously cited, at pp. 112–113. The particular Statute is cited, in legal fashion, as 43 Elizabeth, c.4 (1601).

or redemption of prisoners or captives, and for aide or ease of any poore inhabitants concerning paymente of fifteenes, [and] settinge out of souldiers and other taxes.

(It is of some wry interest that worthy ends not enumerated in the Statute have been held to be invalid charitable trusts by some courts, though in context the original entries were clearly examples, and that bequests that use such terms as "philanthropic" or "benevolent," even if (redundantly) linked with "charitable" in the language of a will have been held to be too broad to qualify as proper charitable trusts. It is perhaps not unreasonably parochial to note that that kind of nonsense is less common in American jurisdictions than in England.[19] This may help to explain the rather radically reduced discretion of the courts in philanthropic dispositions now prevailing in England, discussed a little later.)

Actions in Chancery courts were actions "in equity" rather than "in law." This had the effect (and in part the purpose) not only of secularizing the administration of charitable endowments, but also of removing them from the precedents of feudal custom. That the removal was not total is symbolized by references to trustees as feoffees[20] (meaning originally a conditional grant of property—normally land—for the use of another in return for various feudal duties). The distinction between law and equity has lost most of its significance with the establishment of courts of general jurisdiction. Moreover, precedent came to have the same importance in equitable actions as those actions technically "in law."

It would have been pleasant, and properly consoling to the sociologist seeking common origins as well as common structures and outcomes, had there been a rather unitary law of trusts in the Anglo-American legal system. That law, if sensible, would have had to rest on a common fiduciary principle: wise and prudent men would attend to the properties of widows, of orphans, and other incompetent charges of a deceased man of

---

[19] See Marion R. Fremont-Smith, *Foundations and Government: State and Federal Law and Supervision* (New York: Russell Sage Foundation, 1965), especially pp. 55–58.

[20] See W. K. Jordan, previously cited, pp. 113, 219, and *passim*.

substance; men of alleged business acumen and unusual opportunities to gain high returns would accept, indeed welcome, contributions of other investors, and establish "trusts" for collective
investment; men of substance and charitable impulse would
establish perpetual funds for various worthy causes, and bind
certain trusted individuals and their chosen successors to carry
out their responsibilities.

The law of trusts is not, however, wholly unified; there are
separate and still ambiguous bodies of legal regulations relating
to fiduciary responsibilities. For purposes of quick (though not
absolutely reliable) identification, we may distinguish strictly
private trusts (for named beneficiaries), trusts that have a
charitable intent (without named beneficiaries), and trusts that
simply legalize pooled investments for nothing more laudable
than the mutual financial benefit of participants. Had those
rules evolved from some common legal or customary source,
reference to the regulations as *the law* of trusts would make
some sense. What is common to these forms of trusts is that all
concern fiduciary relationships. Those relations, we have seen,
are considerably broader than what is conventionally treated
as the law of trusts.

Both in origin and current use, the closest relation is that between private and charitable trusts, which do not differ in the
duties of trustees but rather in the mode of enforcement and in
certain exemptions for charitable trusts that we shall explore.
Since we are interested in the current conduct of charitable
trusts, peculiarities of historical origin are consequential only
if they have explanatory value in current practice. Genetic (that
is, historical) explanations of current policies and procedures
would have little value if they stopped at that. Forms may persist while their original rationale has become meaningless. In
the law of trusteeship persistence is real, and thus guides current action.

Public Supervision of Private Trusts. A leading legal problem,
early and late, has been that of public supervision of charitable
trusts.[21] The Chancery courts could themselves initiate action if

----

[21] The leading authority on the law of trusts is Austin W. Scott, *The Law*

trustees were failing in their duties, or if the purposes of the trust were no longer in the public interest. In most American jurisdictions the courts retain that authority. However, courts as such generally lack investigatory staffs, and the prime supervisory duty became that of the attorney general. Here a further difficulty arises, particularly in the United States. Attorneys general also have other duties, and unless the common-law principle has been reaffirmed by statute, many of them may be too inadequately versed in the law of charitable trusts to perform this responsibility. Getting the attention of the attorney general is likely to be difficult, for the layman, too, is obviously ignorant of the law. In the case of charitable trusts and corporations, with unnamed beneficiaries, there are likely to be no true "parties at interest," even if all concerned were suitably knowledgeable and proficient.

Attempts to tighten and rationalize public supervision of charitable trusts have produced a pair of anomalies. In England, the home of the common law, and of Chancery courts for actions in equity, much of the supervision of charitable trusts has passed from the attorney general and courts to administrative agencies: the Ministry of Education and the Charity Commissioners.[22] Both of these agencies have considerable discretionary authority in changing the donor's purposes, in combining endowments and the like without judicial *cy pres* action. (The *cy pres* doctrine is to the effect that if the purposes of a trust cannot be fulfilled, or sensibly fulfilled, or would be against public interest, the trustees or the attorney general must present to the court a "scheme" that will be a worthy purpose as close as possible to the donor's original intent.) Not all American legal jurisdictions even recognize the *cy pres* doctrine, though in some the doctrine of *deviation* has been extended to include a change of purpose. Technically,

---

of Trusts, 2nd ed. (Boston: Little, Brown & Co., 1956). A much more concise review of the law of charitable trusts is provided by Marion R. Fremont-Smith, previously cited.

[22] Our source for this interpretation is again the work of Marion R. Fremont-Smith. The current English legislation and practice, some of it dating only since a legislative reform in 1960, incorporates many recommendations of a Parliamentary Committee, chaired by Lord Nathan. See Committee on the Law and Practice relating to Charitable Trusts, *Report*, Cmd. 8710 (London: H. M. Stationery Office, 1952).

cy pres refers to a change of purpose of a charitable trust, whereas deviation refers to some administrative provision of the trust instrument (such as number and selection of trustees, investments permitted, and the like).[23] A good example of a vain appeal to the principle of deviation was provided by the attempt of the trustees of The Duke Endowment to be relieved of the requirement of keeping its original investments in the Duke Power Company. The North Carolina courts[24] held that the relative hardship of being barred from possibly more advantageous investments was not great enough to warrant a deviation.

Among those jurisdictions where the courts at least nominally recognize the *cy pres* doctrine, or will extend the doctrine of deviation to include purpose, there is a substantial variation in the willingness of the courts actually to exercise discretionary powers. Strict construction, both as to purpose and as to procedure, is the general rule. In American practice, as in England, court action is relatively rare, given the great number of charitable trusts of all sorts. The American anomaly is that the principal policeman of foundations has become a tax-collecting agency, the Internal Revenue Service. That agency, too, has other duties, which are likely to be far more rewarding in terms of tax revenues, and, in any event, the privilege of tax exemption is not the crucial issue with respect to most charitable foundations. Abuse of tax exemption (such as engaging in an unrelated business) is among the least of the ways foundations and similar organizations may fail in proper performance of their philanthropic missions.

Some early difficulties in the clarification of the law of charitable trusts are of sufficient continuing relevance to warrant brief examination. One potential difficulty has been the "rule against perpetuities." According to this rule, a private trust for specified beneficiaries may not run more than 21 years after the death of the last beneficiary living at the time the trust is established. The rule, which is related to the mortmain rules next discussed, is technically that "no real property interest shall vest

---

[23] See Marion R. Fremont-Smith, previously cited, pp. 78–79, 91–93.

[24] The final decision is represented in Cocke v. Duke University 260, N.C. 1, 131 S.E. 2d 909 (1963).

after 21 years after the end of a life in being at the creation of the interest." It is not precisely true that charitable trusts and foundations are exempt from the rule, for the rule technically is not against the duration of a trust but against remoteness of vesting. Yet the nuances of the law are such that it is approximately true that charitable perpetuities are exempt, and certainly true that there is nothing illegal about self-perpetuating boards of trustees.[25] The presumed rationale for the rule is the avoidance of perpetual trusts in family lines. The rule is waived for charitable trusts for unnamed beneficiaries. Here the presumed safeguards are public supervision, including *cy pres* action if warranted.

A second difficulty in legal clarification might be called the "specter of mortmain," that is, the permanent removal of property from the market and its use determined by a "dead hand." Yet the safeguards already noted also apply here. Moreover, the perceived evil of mortmain originally was the perpetual removal of *land* from the market, and its holding by *corporations*. The post-Reformation charitable bequests tended to be money and intangibles (though land-rents might also be part of a bequest). Trustees were often given the discretionary power to buy and sell properties or equities, and courts could order release from specific limitations by the donor.[26]

The discretion of trustees is limited by several enduring principles. Perhaps the most basic one is the duty of *loyalty*. Loyalty is due to the *terms* of the trust and thus, at least inferentially and indirectly, to the donor. Loyalty is also due to the *purposes* of the trust and thus, again at least inferentially and indirectly, to the intended beneficiaries. (Note, however, that the beneficiaries, being unnamed at least as individuals, rarely have a basis for insisting on loyal performance. The proper conduct of the trustee comes from his own integrity, his responsibility to peers, or from outside authority.)

The further implication of the duty of loyalty is the avoidance of self-serving at the expense of the intended beneficiaries.

---

[25] See Robert J. Lynn, "Perpetuities: The Duration of Charitable Funds and Foundations," *UCLA Law Review*, vol. 13, May, 1966, pp. 1074–1099.

[26] See W. K. Jordan, previously cited, p. 121.

There are, of course, certain gray areas of conduct where mild degrees of self-serving do not effectively damage the interests of beneficiaries. But, unlike the director of a business corporation, the trustee is expected to have a *disinterested* dedication to his duties. What we encounter, then, is the duty of loyalty to a charitable principle.

For most foundations (as well as the endowments of educational and other organizations) the duty of loyalty applies to the collectivity of trustees *in perpetuity*. Thus after the initial trustees have been replaced, their successors are expected to be backward-looking by being attentive to precedent, but also forward-looking with a view to adaptation to changing conditions.

Somewhat more than incidentally, the idea of a perpetual endowment is still subject to query, for it does raise some time-honored questions: (a) the problem, akin to mortmain, that properties held in trust may not be fully subject to market transfers; (b) the question of obsolescence of functions, and thus the problem of getting *cy pres* action; (c) the subtler question as to whether it is reasonable to permit a kind of worldly immortality to donors, laying upon future generations of trustees the duty of carrying out of purposes that may still possibly be commendable but increasingly unimportant; and (d) the problem that the rapid growth of foundations and their assets, along with other perpetuities accumulated by colleges and other organizations, may lead to unreasonable economic concentration—the specter of mortmain once more.

The wider the discretion accorded to trustees both in the management of resources and in the selection of beneficiaries, the greater the importance of another principle of proper conduct by trustees: they have the duty to act *prudently*. Known in law as the "prudent man doctrine," the idea is simply that trustees should conduct foundation or similar affairs with circumspection. They are supposed to avoid excesses of speculative risks, excesses of caution, and even excesses of loyalty to the donor's original wisdom. Obviously, criteria of prudence may vary in time and place, as well as in the judgment of conscientious individuals. The fact that boards of trustees are collegial bodies has at least the potential merit of a collective determination of what constitutes prudence. (It may be noted in passing that the authority and responsibilities of foundation trustees are not substantially different whether the foundation is organized as a charitable trust, strictly speaking, or as a charitable corporation.[27] Since charitable corporations have no stockholders, 'the accountabilities of their trustees or directors remain public, not private.)

There remain some critical issues in the law and practice of trusteeship. One set of issues relates to the assurance of responsible stewardship. Since trustees are normally organized into collegia of various sizes, gross misfeasance or malfeasance would require an improbable conspiracy to go unchallenged. Nonfeasance is more difficult to deal with, for that may be the result of mere lethargy and neglect. And since potential beneficiaries normally have no standing in court, about the only course of action available to someone knowledgeable and aggrieved at inaction or inadequate action would be an appeal to the attorney general to intercede. He may be too busy, or too ignorant, to comply with the request.

The stewardship of foundation trustees relates not alone to the management of assets and the assurance of income for current grants and operations. Within the discretionary limits permitted by the foundation's charter and relevant laws, trustees are also responsible for disposing of the income. The prudent man doctrine relates to property management, not to expenditures of income. Thus trustees of unexceptionable prudence in the technical sense may still allow (or even foster) expenditure of income on trivial or frivolous projects. The restraints on such irresponsibility derive more from collective judgment (often involving salaried staff as well as trustees) than from any realistic threat of suit or prosecution. It is the principle of *loyalty* to honorable and charitable purposes that applies to sensible expenditures. How the decisions are made is discussed in some detail in the accompanying essay by Dr. Young.

A further aspect of responsible stewardship is the duty, again shared by trustees and the attorney general, to keep the uses of an endowment from becoming impossible or mischievous. In the United States the attorneys general have commonly failed

---

[27] See Marion R. Fremont-Smith, previously cited, especially pp. 154–157.

in this duty, except in a few jurisdictions (notably California and New York) where definite statutory provision has been made for regular reporting on the part of foundations. Trustees themselves may be laggard in their responsibility to seek permission to update the purposes for which funds may be responsibly used. And American courts have perhaps too much respect for the whims of donors and too little respect for the public interest, which alone would justify original tax exemptions and the current and enduring management of perpetual funds in a changing world.

Critical as one may be of the performance of some trustees, and even of some boards of trustees, one must note that their record of public-spirited (or philanthropic) service has been remarkable. Jordan, writing of some long-established charitable trusts in England, notes some failures of trustees to keep current with economic (or other) changes, yet on net judgment makes an appraisal that deserves partial quotation:

> This large group of trusts is in average terms well over three centuries old. For the most part, the trust instruments were drawn before the law of charitable trusts was well formulated and before men of the western world had gained much experience in the administration of this extraordinary legal and social instrumentality. Most of these trusts were relatively quite small, many very small indeed, and most of them were entrusted to laymen possessed of no particular administrative experience or financial sagacity. None the less, so important has society conceived their purposes to be, so competent were the safeguards erected by the Elizabethan legislation, and so faithful has been the unbroken succession of unpaid and almost unnoticed feoffees that over this long span of time only 174 of the total number of these trusts [2121] have been lost, through negligence, or malfeasance, or merger with other funds. This means, of course, that only 8 per cent of these trusts have disappeared; that perpetuity has in fact been largely achieved even for the smallest and most eccentric of these many endowments. . . .[28]

> But fire, pestilence, wars, and panics have not over a long span of three centuries seriously impeded good and faithful men as they have discharged with brilliance and steady purposefulness social burdens laid on them by men they never

---

[28] See W. K. Jordan, previously cited, p. 123.

knew, but who like them were charged with a vision of a fairer habitation for all mankind.[29]

Trusteeship, resting upon a set of legal principles and restraints that have evolved over several centuries, also represents special applications of a broader class of fiduciary relations and the remarkable principle of lay control over matters of public interest and welfare.

Given the severe restraints on self-dealing, the minimal indirect benefits to business or professional careers from trustee service, the generally nominal or nonexistent payment for service, one must credit the assumption, argued previously, that trustees, too, are likely to be charitably disposed. And the generally effective operation of this remarkable combination of institutional principles clearly owes more to the conscientious and mutually reinforced sharing of these principles than to formal regulation and supervision.

Trusteeship, uniting distinct but compatible institutional principles, preserves an area of discretionary social action that is in considerable measure independent of both the marketplace and the political considerations appropriate to the state. It is a curious, and on close examination, a generally heartening phenomenon.

---

[29] *Ibid.*, p. 125.

Trustees and Foundation Management

Donald R. Young

Trustees and Foundation Management

Donald R. Young

THE EVOLUTION OF THE LAW, LORE, AND CUSTOMARY PRACTICES
of trusteeship provides both a tangle of technical rules and
a very considerable area of discretion for trustees, the custodians
of assets destined for the benefit of others. The discretionary
powers and privileges will inform this entire essay, along with
debatable issues and dubious practices. The discussion that
follows will range over a variety of subjects that relate to the
proper, and improper conduct of philanthropic foundations.
Attention will be given first to the characteristics and responsibilities of trustees in their custody and care of funds entrusted to
their management and appropriate distribution. The discussion
then moves on to such major issues in trustee responsibility and
foundation policy as what programs, agencies, or projects will
be supported; sources of information and advice in making decisions, including salaried staffs; financial policies and administration; and problems of propriety in actual foundation programs.

Trustees and Their Responsibilities

Untold thousands of American men and substantially fewer
women give of their time and talent to the oversight and man-

agement of funds destined for philanthropic purposes. These trustees, mostly drawn from the world of business management and the professions, accept responsibilities comparable to other unpaid public service, such as service on public school boards. Indeed, some individuals may serve in a variety of fiduciary positions. They are motivated, in the main, by genuine public concern, which may be mixed with honorable interest in power and prestige. The primary attention here to foundation trustees and their responsibilities should not cloud the circumstance that they are a portion of a much larger class of trustees and of others who exercise comparable fiduciary responsibilities.

Interest and Self-Interest. Although the fiduciary responsibilities and functions of the trustees of a foundation in the abstract are analogous to those of the directors of a business or manufacturing corporation, there is a significant distinction regarding the extent to which the serving of self-interest is considered proper. The public takes it for granted that a directorship of a profit-making corporation somehow or other will be financially advantageous beyond the stated stipend and is not critical so long as there is no illegal behavior or disadvantage to the stockholders who have given their trust. It also is taken for granted that practically all of those who seek high public office do so for personal advantage as well as because of a desire to serve their fellow citizens, although the elected official or appointed administrator is supposed to be especially circumspect in the use of public funds. Serving self-interest in foundation management, however, even though it may be done legally by acceptance of pay for trustee service or in arms-length transactions of benefit both to the foundation and to the trustee, is questioned by many.

The pervasiveness of this questioning of trustee compensation is evidenced by the fact that the large majority of foundations offer no compensation to their trustees. The most they do is meet out-of-pocket expenses incurred for attendance at meetings or when on foundation business. About half a dozen of the larger foundations pay their trustees substantial amounts of between $25,000 and $35,000. Another dozen or so of the larger foundations pay more modest sums ranging between $1,000 and $20,000. Of the smaller foundations, a few offer token fees of a few hundred dollars and a smaller number pay amounts large enough to be regarded as significant compensation. Some of these foundations are organized as trusts rather than as non-profit corporations and the amount paid trustees is that allowed under state trust law. The Internal Revenue Service raises no objection to the payment of fees to trustees if they are not un-reasonable in relation to the amount of time and effort required, a matter of opinion and actual doubt in the case of several foundations.

The view of the Internal Revenue Service about the compen-sation of foundation trustees seems reasonable, yet a wide-spread critical attitude persists. Payment for the oversight of philanthropic activities is not in the American tradition. The trustees of educational institutions ranging from the public schools to universities and of health and welfare agencies tradi-tionally receive no compensation. Yet the oversight of such in-stitutions and agencies commonly requires more time and effort than does the management of a foundation, for the reason that a foundation is less likely to conduct an extensive operating pro-gram. However, it is in the American tradition to compensate trustees of trust funds, and this may have led to the payment of the trustees of a few foundations organized as trusts. The fact that there are any foundations paying substantial fees to trustees appears to be explained by the circumstance that the present-day foundation is a relatively new arrival on the Ameri-can philanthropic scene, and not yet quite regarded as a full-fledged member of the charitable community.

Experience has shown that it is not necessary to pay founda-tion trustees in order to obtain the services of men of the highest quality. The Rockefeller Foundation, one of the oldest of the larger foundations with a superior record of achievement, has never offered compensation to its trustees, yet the list of those who have served on its board is a veritable list of men of accom-plishment and distinction. The trustees of Carnegie Corporation of New York originally received $5,000 each per year, but they themselves soon voted to end these payments. The giant of all American foundations, The Ford Foundation, pays its trustees an annual stipend of $5,000, a sum that in relation to the mag-nitude of their task and to the distinction of its trustees must be regarded as no more than a token payment rather than as a persuasive argument for service. Even the smaller foundations, such as Russell Sage Foundation, the Milbank Memorial Fund, the New York Foundation, and innumerable others have had no difficulty in securing the unpaid services of trustees of the calibre desired. It may be argued that foundation trustees are worthy of their hire and should not be imposed upon in the name of charity. It is difficult to see that such an argument has any more validity in the case of foundation trustees than it would if applied to those who direct the operations of colleges and universities, welfare agencies, hospitals, museums, or religious bodies.

Dedicated and unrequited service of trustees of foundations as well as of the multitude of other nonprofit agencies rests on a variety of traditional supports. In the American way of life a sense of social responsibility and personal integrity are highly valued. It is a rare individual who would not obtain a pleasurable feeling of satisfaction from participation in a philanthropic accomplishment. Esteem and recognition normally are a valued reward for unselfish service in the interests of mankind. There is always the serious threat of potential disapproval by those whose esteem is desired should fiduciary conduct not measure up to expectations. Further, should informal rewards and penalties fail to restrain those who hold fiduciary positions from violating their trust, the sanctions of the law are ever present. The exceedingly rare recourse to the law because of violations of fiduciary obligations by trustees of foundations and other charitable agencies testifies to the strength of American humanitarian values and to the commonplace acceptance of social responsibilities in the American social order.

The Qualities of Trustees. Of course, there are gross variations in individual qualities of spirit and ability suitable for philanthropic trusteeship. Thus there always is a troublesome problem of selection when a board is to be created or a vacancy to be filled. Just what is to be looked for when an individual is under consideration? Speaking for The Rockefeller Foundation, of which he was then president, Dean Rusk told the House of Representatives Select Committee to Investigate Tax-Exempt

Foundations and Comparable Organizations that "The nominating committee is expected to find men of broad experience, of great capacity, men who are well educated and familiar with the world of affairs, men who have time enough to give to the business of the organization itself and to carry out their responsibility as trustees, and men who have demonstrated in their public record that they have a genuine concern for the well-being of mankind, which is the basic purpose of the organization."[1] Possibly no one would disagree with this description of a good candidate for a foundation trusteeship. It is, however, far too general to determine the selection of a particular person from the multitude who meet its broad criteria. There must be additional criteria, perhaps difficult or even embarrassing to put into words, of greater specificity and more direct relevance to the individual foundation to aid in naming a particular person.

The various more specific criteria that actually, if frequently unconsciously, come into play naturally have varying relevance to the work of any particular foundation. All may be criticized or defended, depending on one's assumptions about efficient foundation management and the role of foundations in American society. For example, a common criticism is that foundations with wide-reaching national or international programs have a tendency to select their trustees from a restricted locality, particularly New York City and the northern Atlantic seaboard states. This has been defended on the ground that trustees need to be readily available for board and committee meetings and that, after all, there is the greatest concentration of suitable persons in those states, many of whom were born and reared elsewhere. The response is that the airplane has made persons in all parts of the country available and that there are suitable persons in all parts of the country, although perhaps less numerous in some regions, who are needed to give broader perspective in foundation operations. Whatever the merits of the argument, large foundations do seem to be drawing a few trustees from greater distances than in the past, a change per-

---

[1] *Hearings Before the Select Committee* (Cox) *to Investigate Tax-Exempt Foundations and Comparable Organizations*, 82nd Congress, 2nd Session, House of Representatives (Washington: Government Printing Office, 1953), pp. 79–80.

haps no less advantageous in terms of public relations than in breadth of perspective. The smaller foundations with largely local programs, of course, have been commended rather than criticized for the selection of local residents as trustees, although it could be argued that they may be especially in need of a less restricted and provincial view of the problems with which they deal than many of them exhibit.

The more detailed qualifications commonly of significance in the selection of foundation trustees in addition to geographic availability fall into two general categories, collegiality, perhaps more simply considered to be congeniality, and skill and experience relevant to a foundation's program.

In order to be effective, the board of trustees of a foundation should meet the definition of a collegial group, as an organized body of men who, as such, have accepted common objectives and duties. Initially most foundations, and particularly the smaller ones, achieve collegiality through the choice by the donor, who usually includes himself, of one or more members of his family, his friends, and business associates and perhaps one or more admired outstanding citizens or professional specialists. Cultural and educational background are likely to be of importance in the selection process, as is also ideological compatibility. Collegiality is also enhanced by the selection of individuals who have had better than average success in their careers and consequently are unlikely to attempt to take personal advantage of a trusteeship if only for the reason that they have little or no need for extra material rewards. These are all natural bases for the initial selection of trustees and not a matter for categorical criticism, particularly in view of the fact that a foundation in the beginning is simply a device for the convenient philanthropic expenditure of private funds that could have been spent for anything from charity to profligate living on the basis of personal whim.

Similar criteria of collegiality continue to be influential in the selection of trustees after the donor is no longer on the scene, but with the exceptions that ordinarily there is a rapidly diminishing regard for former business associates and friends of the donor. Relatives of the donor then also are less likely to be elected as trustees. Direct descendants and widows sometimes are favored, possibly on the doubtfully justifiable ground that foundation money otherwise would have been theirs. There is, however, a more persuasive, but far from definitive, argument for giving the responsibility of a trusteeship to the descendant of a donor in that an extra sense of obligation to pursue his forebear's objective because of affection and earlier association may be assumed. Although often contrary to universalistic criteria of selection, kinship and lineage have never been totally displaced as honorable principles of social placement in our traditions. In conformity with universalistic principles, it has become increasingly difficult to inherit a particular social position —even in "family-dominated" corporations such as Ford Motors or the DuPont Corporation. It is not by any means unknown.

The continuation of heirs and descendants of the donor on a foundation's board of trustees also may be viewed cynically, or at least pragmatically. The family fortune may not have been exhausted by the original gift or bequest, and heirs to the remainder of the original fortune may see fit to supplement the foundation's capital by additional donations.

The other types of criteria of collegiality almost universally continue to operate in the selection of foundation trustees, but as the composite character of a foundation board and its activities inevitably are modified over time, the substantive natures of the cultural, educational, and ideological requirements for compatibility also are modified. The prevailing collegiality of foundation boards is easy to attack as being in the nature of an exclusive club and unrelated to the socially and legally approved objectives of foundations. The only defense, and it is one with merit, is that team effort rather than a babel of tongues is required for effective operation.

Team effort, however, is not enough for effective operation, for that could be too cozy for effective decision. The second set of criteria for foundation trusteeship is that of relevant skill and experience. Despite the prevailing American tradition of lay trusteeship for philanthropic organizations, discussed in Wilbert Moore's preceding essay, there is great need for trustee understanding and expertise in the areas both of foundation management and of program operation. Across the range of boards of trustees (including those of foundations) there are many examples of transitional situations in which the boards essentially consist of two collegial groups, surviving in a situation of uneasy truce or unstable tension. The one group comprises the family, friends, and former business or professional associates of the original donor. The other comprises members chosen for their trained competence or experience relevant to the primary goals of the organization's program. The overt manifestations of strain between these collegia are likely to be genteel, but real.

A foundation's ordinary management requirements include at least some degree of sophistication if not expertness in finance, law, and business administration. The larger the foundation the more obvious and pressing is the need for these skills. Few would maintain that they are not desirable and few foundation boards are entirely lacking in this respect. Businessmen and corporation executives, bankers and investment specialists, and lawyers constitute the great majority of foundation trustees. The laity is not to be viewed as a cross-section of the local or national community.

Less clear in the minds of foundation donors and trustees in general is any need for trustee representation at the professional level of the areas of foundation program operation. Foundation trustees are not commonly chosen because they represent potential beneficiaries in the direct sense of specialization in their fields or of personal identification with the classes of possible recipients of aid. Program development and the selection of beneficiaries are considered adequately managed by lay review of areas of philanthropic opportunities and of individual applications with the aid of such supporting testimony as may be offered or such advice of staff or independent consultants as may be thought desirable. This simple procedure no doubt works very well for a foundation that restricts its activities to a community or limited region with which its trustees are intimately familiar, particularly if grants mainly are made to well-established organizations. It also can work very well for a foundation with a more wide-ranging and venturesome program if it has been fortunate in securing a competent staff, but, even so, it is advantageous to have one or more trustees able to ask penetrating questions based on personal experience or professional knowledge. Otherwise the board must be content with confining itself to very broad policy decisions and almost routine approval of staff proposals. It is risky to assume that a foundation board, merely because of local residence, is familiar with a community's philanthropic needs or even of the relative needs and merits of well-established philanthropic organizations. Only a very few foundations, even among the larger ones, have seen fit to employ a staff professionally so competent that their trustees may with confidence rely on their technical judgments, without knowledgeable questioning.

The growing desirability that foundation boards include men who are experienced or professionally competent in the fields of foundation operation is a consequence of two developments of the present century. First, the great concentrations of population in which most foundations are active have made it difficult if not impossible to assemble boards that have thorough familiarity with philanthropic needs and opportunities for the wise expenditure of the funds at their disposal. Second, all fields of philanthropic endeavor have passed from the stage when humane largesse was adequate to one in which accumulated knowledge about effective procedures for amelioration and prevention of suffering and social inadequacy must be taken into account. A sense of social responsibility and generous devotion of time and money to human welfare are as necessary and praiseworthy as ever in philanthropic endeavor, but they no longer are enough, if they ever were, for maximum accomplishment.

A second kind of knowledge relevant to a foundation's program requires consideration for board representation. Should there be one or more representatives of the major categories of potential beneficiaries? It is not unusual for college or university presidents, professors, or trustees to serve on the boards of foundations concerned with higher education and research, and the ministry in the case of programs concerned with religion, or medical men if there is an interest in health. There is strong argument for expanding this practice in these three fields and in other areas where it is less common, such as family and child welfare agencies, museums, or organizations concerned with international relations. There is, however, a common fear that such representatives, while conceded to have much to contribute to trustee deliberations, may attempt to take advantage of their position to secure grants for their own agencies, a much exaggerated fear that still has some justification in experience. In any event, it is a reflection on the selection process and on the behavior of other trustees if an unjustifiable grant is made to an agency with which any trustee is identified. It cannot be denied that a trustee-favored agency has an advantage, but it does not follow that this is invariably or even usually a matter for criticism. The nuances of this situation are worth exploring briefly. Blatant and improper advocacy by a trustee is likely to lead to genteel rejection by his colleagues, with overtones of condemnation for a kind of self-serving interest (though commonly without personal, material benefit—that would be unsufferable). To avoid any hint of conflict of interest, at the other extreme, the trustee may conspicuously absent himself from deliberations on a proposal. The by-laws of The Rockefeller Foundation, for example, provide that "During the consideration of a proposed appropriation by the board of trustees or a committee thereof, any trustee who is officially connected with the prospective beneficiary shall withdraw from the meeting until the vote has been taken; but his withdrawal shall not be deemed to affect the existence of a quorum."[2] Of course, this scarcely diminishes a trustee's influence. In the ideal situation, which is not rare, the trustee's special concern leads to unusual care in examining the application, and, if it is approved, unusual care in overseeing the actual operation of the program financed. Naturally, the applicant may be grateful for the friend in court in passing on his proposal, and somewhat less grateful for the special concern his patron demonstrates after he has obtained the requested funds.

Question may be raised about the desirability of electing as a trustee a person already serving on the board of one or more other foundations. There is some fear of the charge of a foundation "interlock" which has been raised in Congress and elsewhere. Quite a number of persons do serve as trustees of two foundations, a much smaller number on the boards of three or more. In the mid-1960's in New York, out of a total of something short of 3,000 foundation trustees, 359 were serving on two or

---

[2] F. Emerson Andrews, *Legal Instruments of Foundations* (New York: Russell Sage Foundation, 1958), p. 212.

more boards at an average of 2.2 foundation trusteeships per person. Out of a total of 357 trustees in Wisconsin, 88 were serving on two or more boards. In Texas there were 40 multiple trustees out of a total of 639. Most foundations involved in multiple trusteeships are relatively small. Frequently they have trustees in common because they have the same or related donors or rely on the same legal or financial counselor serving as a trustee. The interlocking of foundations by means of multiple trusteeship is insignificant for the obvious reasons that the prevailing adherence to the principle of management by laymen disparages the value of experience, foundation objectives differ widely, independence of action is highly valued, and with relatively few exceptions trustee service is uncompensated. There is no moral or legal reason that the same person should not serve on more than one foundation's board, but in such cases proper attention to duties can be burdensome. The larger foundations generally do not select as trustees persons already serving on the board of a large foundation, but do not seem to mind dual service if the other is small.

It is often urged that foundation boards should include more individuals chosen from a number of population elements at present grossly underrepresented, particularly Negroes, Jews, Catholics, women, and labor. A common view is that foundation funds are tax-exempt trusts for public benefit and consequently should be managed by trustees broadly representative of the public. There is, of course, no justification whatever for discriminating against a member of any population element because of that membership. Conversely, there is no justification for imposing the responsibilities of foundation trusteeship on a member of any identifiable group or interest merely because of that membership and without regard for the qualities and abilities necessary to fulfill the responsibilities. In fact, the election to trusteeship of an individual materially less well equipped to meet the accompanying obligations than his colleagues reduces the effectiveness of the board and has an unfortunate tendency to lower esteem for his group in general. There is merit in the view that foundation trustees should be drawn from a variety of population elements, but only if due weight is given to relevant individual qualities. Certainly there often is special merit in the view that a foundation actively concerned with the condition of a particular element in the population should include among its trustees some proportion of qualified individuals identified with that element. A board of trustees composed exclusively, or primarily, of all-purpose public representatives would have all the difficulties of a national commission or political party. The female Negro labor-leader, mother of two, from the Southwest and married to a Mexican-American Catholic, may have personal talents or knowledge relevant to a foundation's activities. None of her "demographic" qualifications necessarily leads to that assumption.

Modes of Selecting Trustees. In the absence of any clear consensus on the specific qualities required for effective trustee service other than such general criteria as those offered in the previously quoted testimony of Dean Rusk, the manner of selection is of determining importance. The ordinary foundation board is a cooptive, self-perpetuating body. This is true even in the state of greatest concentration of foundations, New York, where it is a legal requirement that the trustees of a nonprofit corporation, the most common form of foundation organization, must be elected by the members of the corporation, for the members and trustees commonly are the same individuals. State laws concerning the selection of trustees of foundations both in corporate and in trust form vary, as do the relevant provisions of certificates of incorporation, by-laws, and instruments of trust,[3] but self-perpetuation is the general rule. Self-perpetuation, however, is widely viewed with suspicion by the general public as undemocratic and liable to misuse when fiduciary responsibilities are involved. A minority of foundations attempt to meet such questions by a variety of provisions for the selection of trustees other than by cooption.

A few foundations guard against the possibility of a self-perpetuating clique with limited philanthropic vision unresponsive to changing opportunities by requiring that trustees be the in-

---

[3] A well-selected compilation of such documents is F. Emerson Andrews' *Legal Instruments of Foundations* (New York: Russell Sage Foundation, 1958), 318 pp.

cumbents of specified positions or that trustee vacancies be filled by action of such incumbents. An early example of such a requirement in a codicil of the will of Benjamin Franklin provided that a bequest of 1,000 pounds in trust to the inhabitants of Boston "be managed under the direction of the Select Men united with the ministers of the oldest Episcopalian, Congregational and Presbyterian Churches in that town."[4] As another example, the trustees of the Trexler Foundation are appointed by the President Judge of the Orphans Court Division of the Court of Common Pleas of Lehigh County, Pennsylvania, in accordance with the will of the donor. The finances of community trusts are managed by local banks as trustees with provision for the allocation of funds for charitable purposes by distribution committees composed mainly of representatives of relevant community interests selected by incumbents of specified positions such as judges and the mayor. Trustees of foundations established by business and manufacturing corporations with very few exceptions are directors or officers of the parent corporation, and understandably so since their philanthropies must be of some benefit, however slight, to the corporation. The trustees of federal foundations, the National Science Foundation and the National Foundation on the Arts and the Humanities, with its two cooperating entities, the National Endowment for the Arts and the National Endowment for the Humanities, are appointed by the President with informal advice from leaders in the fields of operation and the consent of the Senate. It is easy to think of innumerable other workable ways for avoiding cooption, ranging from the external suggestion of panels of suitable candidates to the simple appointment by the holders of specified public or private positions or by election by a designated organization such as a religious, charitable, educational, or scientific body. Private schools and universities commonly provide for election of some or all trustees by former students, with nominating committees being presumably attentive to any or all of several considerations: (a) achieved eminence in a business, artistic, or profes-

---

[4] Robert H. Mulreany, "Foundation Trustees: Selection, Duties, and Responsibilities," *UCLA Law Review*, vol. 13, May, 1966, p. 1053.

sional field; (b) possible qualifications for sensible counsel; (c) current or prospective substantial financial support for the university.

We have encountered one situation, which is probably not unique, in which the donors to a nonprofit organization comprise the eligible electors of trustees. The Community Hospital of Princeton, New Jersey, has an annual election of trustees, and the eligible electorate consists of those who have contributed five dollars or more to the hospital's support during the preceding year. It is scarcely surprising that there is rarely a contest and the incumbent trustees normally are reelected or in effect choose their successors. As mentioned on page 18, at least one foundation follows a similar principle, assigning one voting right for each $1000 of contribution to the foundation's funds. The Richardson Foundation (recently renamed the Smith Richardson Foundation) is organized as a nonprofit corporation. Members of the corporation comprise lineal descendants of Lunsford Richardson and his wife, Mary Lynn Richardson, and their spouses, who are at least 21 years of age and have at least one voting right. Such rights may be acquired by gift or bequest from qualified members, but new rights may be established by additional gifts to the foundation, either on behalf of the giver or on behalf of others who qualify as dependents of their spouses.[5]

Very few foundations use any formula other than the self-perpetuating board. The arrangement is perfectly legal and the advantages in terms of continuity are clear. If silence gives consent, the absence of outcry by legislative committees, public agencies, or self-appointed public spokesmen may indicate that the law and precedent favoring self-perpetuation of trustee boards is not a tender issue. Some of the possible alternatives are scarcely inviting, or sensible. Others might be.

Cooption of trustees to fill vacancies does, indeed, have advantages for foundation management that are difficult, although not impossible, to obtain under other systems of selection. If collegiality of board members is advantageous, as argued earlier, cooption is the simplest way to assure that it is achieved and

---

[5] "Amended Certificate of Incorporation of the Richardson Foundation, Inc.," typescript copy on file at The Foundation Center, New York.

maintained. Teamwork in the effective pursuit of a foundation program requires a considerable degree of continuity of board personnel, most readily assured by cooption, so that there may be sufficient understanding of objectives and a background of experience adequate both for decisions on project proposals and for continuing program planning. The chances of obtaining and maintaining a board with reasonable balance in such matters as age distribution, availability, and relevant skill and experience are improved if vacancies are filled by those who are intimately familiar with its existing composition and supplementary needs. A trustee owing his selection to a person or organization apart from the foundation understandably may feel that he should advocate an interest of his selector not necessarily in harmony with the foundation's objectives and program, perhaps that he should be a spokesman for a position taken by his selector or even that it is his obligation to support favorable action on grant applications in areas with which his selector may be identified. A selective process that has a tendency to divide a trustee's loyalty to his trust is disadvantageous to the foundation. Trustees need wholeheartedly to identify their efforts with the foundation's objectives and program, never to think of the foundation as an instrument to be used in furthering an externally determined purpose. It is a high calling, not always ideally fulfilled.

It may not be argued that all foundations should be cooptive, only that cooption has some advantages in comparison with other selection procedures and that on the whole it has worked very well. In most small foundations, which are commonly no more than convenient mechanisms for personal benevolence, there can scarcely be any effective argument against cooption of trustees. The coopted trustees may, after all, have a new idea, though that idea may not get far. It must be noted that many of the small foundations are only formally cooptive, for the donors during their lifetime normally have, and use, the right of selection of new trustees.

The larger foundations, in the nature of the case, are relatively freer of the donor's personal influence (though the discretion of some trustee boards is very restricted under the original terms of the donor's gift). For most of the larger foundations, self-perpetuating boards have gained in perspective by recruiting new members. The theoretical possibility of "more of the same" has not been the rule, which may say something about the conscience, and conscientiousness, of trustees.

The self-perpetuating board may be effective, beyond reasonable expectations, and still impolitic. Community trusts, for example, could scarcely survive such an arrangement, nor could the federally supported foundations. Other nominally private foundations are required by charter to support parks, playgrounds, or civic development. Still other endowments are designated for educational or charitable fields identified with a specific religious body. It would be highly unlikely that such endowments would be entrusted to a self-perpetuating board of trustees without current representation of the interests invoked or tapped by the fund. They are not. It does not follow that "representative" boards of trustees have easier problems, or that the decisions reached are somehow superior. They are not.

The task of preparing and winnowing a list of potential candidates to fill a trustee vacancy commonly and most efficiently is the responsibility of a committee of trustees appointed for the purpose, although this responsibility also may be assigned to a standing committee such as the executive committee or to an individual, perhaps the chairman or donor, if still living. It is risky to leave the matter to the board as a whole, for it may not be assumed that an adequate canvass of qualified persons will be made if it is no one's particular responsibility. Names supplied by mail or in person in response to a general request for suggestions from the board or brought forward in discussion in a meeting will almost certainly produce a spotty list. Assigned responsibility for a careful search is especially needed if there is a particular gap in board experience and knowledge to be filled. Furthermore, there always is reticence to speak freely in open meeting about a person suggested, however casually, by a colleague, partly for fear of giving offense by criticizing a colleague's friend and partly because of the likelihood of less knowledge about the individual than that possessed by the one who suggested his name. Of course, all board members should be urged to make suggestions to the committee given the responsibility for proposing a winnowed list of candidates, but it must be kept in mind that such suggestions probably will be heavily weighted with business associates and friends and unrepresentative of the wider range of suitable possibilities.

A committee is needed to search out qualified persons not thought of by other board members, and discreetly but carefully to check the qualifications of all who come to their attention. Major staff members should be consulted, for a good working relationship with staff is essential. The staff also may have a better acquaintance than any member of the board with people who are knowledgeable about the area of a foundation's program. There is no need to hurry in filling a vacancy, for obviously it is better to be short-handed for a while than be saddled with an inappropriate trustee. As a rule, it is best for the committee to propose more than one name for a vacancy, possibly in an order of preference, so that the board may not be put in a position of rubberstamping the choice of a minority of its members. Discussion of several candidates believed suitable by the committee—a proper search always may be expected to turn up more than one well-qualified person—may also improve the board's understanding of its total composition and requirements if thoughtful consideration is given the reasons for proposing the particular names before them. A committee on trustee selection may be appointed ad hoc when a vacancy occurs, but there is an advantage in having it as a standing committee so that there may be continual responsibility for thinking about potential candidates and a tentative backlog list to start with when needed.

The several circumstances under which vacancies occur (expiration of a term of office, retirement age, resignation, removal for cause, or death) raise questions that should be answered in the formal legal instruments governing a foundation.

Trustees' terms of office vary from one year to life. It cannot be said that there is any particular optimum period for trustee service, although it could be argued that one extreme is too short for effective service and that the other may be too long for progressive management. It also can be said that usually it takes a year or so for a trustee to gain familiarity with his role and become an effective member of the board. This suggests that perhaps a three- to five-year period period is a sensible minimum term. Reelection for one or more additional terms after initial satisfactory service also seems reasonable. In actual practice, re-election from term to term is routine foundation practice, so that ordinarily a vacancy occurs at the expiration of a trustee's term only in a technical sense. It is, of course, much too embarrassing in a collegial group to drop a sitting trustee and elect a new and untried member in his place to expect it to happen frequently unless obligatory.

If it is thought that practically automatic reelection should be avoided in order to prevent stagnation and provide for fresh trustee perspective, two simple devices are available. One is the adoption of a fixed rule against reelection after one term, or per-haps after two terms if the first is believed too short. Should it be felt that such an absolute rule might deprive the foundation of the continued services of an exceptional trustee who should be kept in office longer than most, provision that former trustees may be reelected after the expiration of a year following a previ-ous term would meet the situation without directly affronting anyone concerned. The second device, much more commonly in use, is a definite age for retirement, possibly 65 or 70. A variant of this device that avoids forcing retirement before a normal term has been completed is to provide that no trustee may be elected after passing a stated birthday. Under such provision, too, the services of a vigorous and progressive trustee may re-grettably be lost. The case of a foundation trustee retired from that office for age who some years later twitted the foundation with the remark that he was still serving, and it may be said with distinction, as a member of the Supreme Court of the United States, comes to mind. As another example, an automatically re-tired foundation trustee who also was a university president later demonstrated his vigor and freshness of mind by innovat-ing leadership in a reorganization program at his institution. Numerous such examples could be cited. Such examples, how-ever, do not meet the point that retirement at a stated age is not solely, and perhaps not primarily, to be defended as a means for getting rid of old fogies, but rather as a device for making room for new minds. Trustees usually are selected well before their approach to 65 or 70, usually in a broadly defined "middle" age, so that practically all have had ample time to make their contribution well before automatic retirement. Nevertheless, it is a difficult and distasteful matter to terminate the unselfish philanthropic services of anyone, whether by individual decision or by fixed rule. In our changing society, however, where the problem areas of foundation opportunity and the means for social amelioration and improvement also are in constant change, foundation boards need to be kept in harmony with the times.

Foundation trustees resign but rarely, and then usually in consequence of some new conflicting obligation. In those instances where a trustee after election finds he really is not interested in the foundation's program or even in opposition to it, perhaps later loses his initial interest, or finds he has no contribution to make, the easy and customary way out is to decline reelection, possibly meanwhile with declining attention to foundation business and avoidance of meetings. Trustees of foundations in corporate form are free to resign at their pleasure, and no more is needed in the governing legal instruments than a simple statement of procedure, such as requiring a letter of resignation addressed to the secretary and formal provision for filling the resulting unexpired term. Resignations and selection of new trustees can be more complicated if a foundation is established as a trust rather than as a corporation. Court approval may be needed, although usually court supervision of the succession of trustees arises only in the case of testamentary trusts, and even with these it can be dispensed with in a majority of states. Most foundations in trust form have been created inter vivos with specific provision for trustee succession. The same provision for filling a vacancy caused by resignation can apply to filling one caused by death.

Termination of a trustee's services for cause has been rare in the history of American foundations. Removal because of a violation of the law applying to foundations is too complicated a matter for discussion by a layman, and in any case it is not a matter for board action beyond the reporting of relevant facts to the proper authorities.

Cause for removal, however, may not be a violation of the law. Failure to meet obligations also should result in termination of a trustee's office. The simplest provision for the accomplishment of this purpose is a rule that any trustee failing to attend some specified number of meetings of the board is automatically

dropped. Such a rule may be eased a bit without being too seriously weakened by the addition of a clause making it inoperable
if a justifying explanation of the absences satisfactory to the
board is offered. To allow for board action in case of inappropriate, although not necessarily illegal, behavior by a trustee,
such as willful obstructionism, gross self-serving bias, or misbehavior in some capacity other than his trusteeship making
him clearly undesirable as a continuing associate, a board should
have considerable discretion concerning the termination of a fellow trustee's services. The trust indenture setting up The Duke
Endowment gives such discretion in the following provision:
"By the affirmative vote of a majority of the then trustees any
officer, and by the affirmative vote of three-fourths of the then
trustees any trustee, may be removed for any cause whatever
at any meeting of the trustees called for the purpose in accordance with the rules and regulations."[6] Whether or not the discretionary powers of removal need to be as broad as those of
the trustees of The Duke Endowment is a moot question, but if
they are, there probably is more reason to fear that they will
be underused rather than misused. At least a board should have
some recourse if a resignation is refused when the resignation
is believed to be to the foundation's advantage by three-fourths
or more of the trustees.

Trustee Duties and Their Enforcement.   The legal responsibilities and liabilities of foundation trustees are specified by the federal and state laws governing nonprofit corporations and trusts
and by the rulings of the Internal Revenue Service. The corporate form of organization has been favored partly because of the
belief that trustee liability was less severe than in the case of
trusts, but today there is little difference if the trust instrument
is drawn with trustee protection in mind. Furthermore, there is
an evident tendency on the part of legislatures and the courts
toward uniformity regarding the responsibilities of trustees of
both forms of organization that is characterized by increasing
strictness in the case of the corporate form and somewhat en-

---

[6] F. Emerson Andrews, *Legal Instruments of Foundations* (New York:
Russell Sage Foundation, 1958), p. 93.

larged discretion for the trustees of foundations in trust form. There is no reason for any differences whatever; those that persist are irrational survivals from originally separate legal origins. The essence of the matter is that, whatever the legal form of a foundation, the fiduciary obligations of the trustees require that there shall be no breach of trust, that the duty of loyalty to the foundation demands the avoidance of possible conflicts of interest, that reasonable care, diligence, and prudence must be exercised in the conduct of a foundation's affairs.

It is anomalous that the Internal Revenue Service of the Treasury Department, a tax-collecting agency of the federal government, is the most active agency in defining and enforcing proper fiduciary behavior by foundation trustees, for all but a very few foundations exist and operate by the authority of the several states. With very few exceptions, however, the states have done little to make certain that the foundations within their jurisdiction are meeting their legal obligations. In 1968 only eleven states had statutes requiring foundation registration and reporting.[7] However, it should be noted that one of these is New York, where 1,822 of the 6,803 foundations holding almost $9,500,000,000 of the not quite $20,000,000,000 total foundation assets as reported in *The Foundation Directory, Edition 3* are located.[8]

State attorneys general have supervisory power but as a rule have shown little interest in using it. The Internal Revenue Service has been able, one might say compelled, to move into this largely neglected area of law enforcement because of its duty to decide whether or not a particular foundation is entitled to federal tax exemption and because of its accompanying authority to establish rules and issue rulings of tax exemption neces-

---

[7] Marion R. Fremont-Smith, *Foundations and Government: State and Federal Law and Supervision* (New York: Russell Sage Foundation, 1965), p. 259; and supplementary memorandum dated February 3, 1969.

[8] *The Foundation Directory, Edition 3* defines a foundation as "a nongovernmental, nonprofit organization having a principal fund of its own, managed by its own trustees or directors, and established to maintain or aid social, educational, charitable, religious, or other activities serving the common welfare." It includes only those making grants of not less than $10,000 in the year of record or having assets of not less than $200,000. F. Emerson Andrews, "Introduction," in Marianna O. Lewis, editor, *The Foundation Directory, Edition 3* (New York: published for The Foundation Library Center by Russell Sage Foundation, 1967), pp. 7, 15–16.

sary for the exemption from federal tax of donations to foundations. All of the rules and actions of the Service are based on
its proper concern that tax exemption be legally justified, but it
can be argued that this concern at times has gone beyond the extreme limits of the ordinary interests of a tax-collecting agency.
For example, a 1965 Treasury Department report on foundations responding to requests of both Houses of the Congress
devotes most of its attention to such seemingly tenuously tax-
related matters as the timing of foundation expenditures, foundation business activities, the voting of foundation stock, foundation investment policies, and the selection of trustees. The
relation of these subjects to federal tax exemption of foundations
and the tax liabilities of donors becomes more understandable
if the more critical wording of the report is quoted. In the same
order, the report lists these subjects as "Delay in benefits to
charity," "Foundation involvement in business," "Family use of
foundations to control corporate and other property," "Financial
transactions unrelated to charitable functions," and "Broaden-
ing of foundation management."[9] It still may be claimed that
these matters, at least not all of them, do not normally fall within
the province of a tax-collecting agency, but that is where they
have fallen.

The extent of the growing supervisory role of the Internal
Revenue Service in foundation affairs is more understandable as
a matter of practical necessity than it is in administrative logic.
The federal government is obligated to make certain that its requirements for tax exemption are enforced. Foundations reduce
federal individual income, gift, and estate tax revenues. Congress has shown both in four legislative investigations of foundations and by enactments such as the Revenue Acts of 1950
and 1964, among others, that it wants the Internal Revenue
Service to define its concern with foundations broadly. Furthermore, there presently is no other federal agency with authority
to concern itself with foundation activities, although it has been
suggested that such authority be given the Department of Health,
Education, and Welfare or that some new agency be created.

---

[9] *Treasury Department Report on Private Foundations* (Washington: Government Printing Office, 1965), p. v.

This would not end the proper interest of the Internal Revenue Service with respect to tax matters, but might transfer responsibility for other matters to an agency primarily concerned, say, with welfare rather than with revenues.

Tax exemption is neither a legal nor a logical basis for Internal Revenue Service oversight of foundations' activities beyond the point of making certain that they are not used as devices for illegal tax evasion and do not support activities other than those specified as proper by act of Congress. This affords the Internal Revenue Service wide investigative latitude, but even so it has been extended beyond clear reason. An example of such extension has been the apparent inclination of the Service unduly to favor foundation grants to other tax-exempt organizations. Another example is insistence that charters make specific provision for the disposition of remaining assets to other philanthropic agencies on possible termination, a matter of more direct concern to the chartering state, as is assured by law in New York. Certainly it is a serious matter that the great majority of states do not require charter provision for ultimate distribution of assets and permit dissolution of foundations with no record of the distribution of funds remaining at the time. In some states there even remains a question of whether they must go to charity. However, the omission of proper state action does not automatically qualify the Internal Revenue Service in law or expertise as the proper guide and supervisor. That the Internal Revenue Service's extensive concept of its foundation responsibilities is not without effect is demonstrated by the excessively cautious counsel of foundation lawyers in general.

It may be said that because the Internal Revenue Service stands alone as a federal foundation watcher there is no choice but to allow and even encourage it to take great latitude in interpretation of its Congressional mandate. This view is defended by noting the fact that most states have paid little attention to their chartered foundations and charitable trusts. A more logical conclusion is that every effort should be made to induce the slack states to meet their responsibilities. Although claiming broad responsibilities for monitoring foundation behavior, the Service has as its only remedy for improper foundation activity the assessment of a tax penalizing potential beneficiaries rather than the initiation of corrective measures, is seriously lacking in experience and staff properly to implement its claims, and actually has been reluctant adequately to carry out its minimum oversight duty, that of reasonable and reasonably frequent audit. The frankly offered defense of this reluctance has been that there is a shortage of auditors and that foundation audits produce additional tax payments far too small to balance the cash returns of auditors if assigned elsewhere. From one point of view, this may be a commendable businesslike attitude, but it does not encourage advocacy of the Service as a foundation watchdog beyond enforcement of tax-related legislation more narrowly defined. The basic question, and one that permits honest debate, is whether the federal government should be the principal monitor of foundations and charitable trusts because their behavior is distantly tax-related, or should primary supervision rest with the states, which have given life to virtually all of these charitable entities. The number of states that definitely make provision for exercising this duty significantly is increasing.

Passing reference that needs amplification has been made to concern by donors and prospective trustees that service as a trustee might be hazardous because of liability for some unblameworthy but, nevertheless, illegal action. Although there is little likelihood that an honest man will get in trouble because of service as a foundation trustee, exculpatory clauses commonly are found in instruments of trust and other documents governing foundations. The Twentieth Century Fund agreement of trust provides that "no trustee hereunder shall be liable for anything except his own personal and willful default or misfeasance."[10] The constitution of Russell Sage Foundation offers an example of a carefully drawn provision limiting the liability of trustees:

> The Foundation shall indemnify any person made a party to any action, suit or proceeding—of any nature whatsoever—by reasons of the fact that he, his testator or intestate, is or was a trustee, officer or employee of the Foundation or of any founda-

---

[10] F. Emerson Andrews, *Philanthropic Giving* (New York: Russell Sage Foundation, 1950), p. 97.

tion or corporation which he served as such at the request of
the Foundation, against the reasonable expenses, including attorney's fees, actually and necessarily incurred by him in connection with the defense of such action, suit or proceeding, or
in connection with any appeal therein, except in relation to
matters as to which it shall be adjudged in such action, suit
or proceeding that such trustee, officer or employee is liable for
negligence or misconduct in the performance of his duties.

Any amount payable by way of indemnity shall be determined
by the Board of Trustees of the Foundation. The Board of
Trustees shall, within the time prescribed by Section 63 of the
New York General Corporation Law, mail a notice to the members of the Foundation setting forth the name or names of the
persons paid, the amounts of the payments and the final disposition of the litigation.

Properly there can be no relief for trustee liability for negligence
or for anything done in bad faith. Otherwise it is reasonable to
limit the liability of trustees and indemnify those who may suffer
unjustifiably because of their service. However broad an exculpatory clause may be permitted in a particular state, an over-
riding factor is the disapproval of the Internal Revenue Service
of any provision exempting a trustee from responsibility for violations of the Internal Revenue Code even in the absence of
negligence or bad faith.

The legal responsibilities of foundation trustees are no more
than a minimum statement of duties. Their meticulous fulfillment does not satisfy the requirements of proper service. They
do go much further than the popular uninformed notion of the
duties of a foundation trustee as attendance at board meetings
at which decisions are made on whatever applications for grants
have been received since the previous meeting. This notion un-
fortunately is practically what happens in too many poorly managed large foundations and also in most personal convenience
foundations, where it is difficult to avoid or criticize because
they are too small to justify the time and cost of a more constructive procedure. There is no excuse, however, for such passive allocations when available funds are sufficient to be of more
constructive philanthropic influence. Trustees of the more generously endowed foundations have responsibilities far exceeding
the simple voting of grants which include: (1) the determination of general operating policies, (2) financial management,

(3) program operation, and (4) continuous program review. No person should accept a foundation trusteeship who is not willing, able, and determined to shoulder his share of these obligations.

It is, of course, both possible and necessary to delegate much of the actual task of foundation operation, but the authority of trustees may not be delegated nor may the responsibility for thorough and constant review of activities be neglected. Nominal trustees are prohibited by law, although in fact they are not uncommon, particularly in family foundations and others where the donor is still alive and active in his foundation's affairs. The attitude toward unilateral donor action that, after all, it is his money, may be understandable, but it also is contrary to the legal and moral principle that directors must direct, that trustees must fulfill their fiduciary responsibilities even though actual management duties are delegated. Trustees with proper modesty may take small credit for the achievements of others with the use of wisely granted funds, but they must take all the blame for anything that goes wrong.

The determination of general operating policies needs to be preceded by a decision on the one or several fields of benevolence in which support will be concentrated. No foundation, not even the giant Ford Foundation, has enough money and staff to be effective in all fields of philanthropic need and endeavor. Any foundation, even one that restricts its activities to a limited geographic area or metropolitan region, will be more effective if it has a consciously ranked priority list of interests. Scatteration of funds is an easy but wasteful procedure that requires no well-worked-out program and has weak, random impact on social needs. A common cliché among foundation administrators is that a chokebore shotgun has more impact on the target than a scattershot, provided, of course, that the aim is true. The choice of fields of activity is wide open to foundations. There is no proper criticism of the selection of any field, although for tax exemption it must fall within one of the allowable categories to be found in the Internal Revenue Code of 1954, mainly in Section 501(c)(3), which lists "religious, charitable, scientific, testing for public safety, literary or educational purposes, or for the prevention of cruelty to children or animals."

There are so innumerably many opportunities for philanthropic investment in the allowable fields that donors and trustees, insofar as the latter are not restricted by the specifications of their charter or instrument of trust, should feel entirely free in their choice. Of course, there will be critics of any choice because of personal conviction that this or that other field is of paramount importance and crucially in need of support. This is a matter of personal judgment and not for authoritative determination. Early foundation support of research on atomic energy and on rockets, for example, could not have been defended or condemned, whichever attitude one may hold today, on any basis recognizably related to consequences experienced years later. It is true that some fields are much more generously financed than others; for example, health in relation to the arts and humanities, or cancer research in relation to research on rheumatic fever. Justified or not, such disparities are largely a consequence of comparative public appeal at a particular time. Who is to say that society would be better off if the distribution of private philanthropic funds were determined in some less democratic manner than by the free choice of donors and their trustee successors?

The Forms of Foundation Aid

With one or more fields decided upon as of primary interest, three categories of operating policy questions come to the fore. Running a foundation requires that a surprising number of policy choices be made about the scope and nature of operations, about financial policy and management, and about decisions concerning program and projects. These policies will and should vary with the size and overall objectives of foundations and will be modified from time to time as personnel and circumstances change. They need not and in fact cannot be made wisely before a foundation is in operation, but rather in the main will be settled in the course of experience in action. In no case other than in matters of law and ethics is there a flat right or wrong policy applicable to all foundations.

Perhaps the first question on scope and nature of operations, whatever the field of operation, is whether grants mainly will be relatively passive allocations to established and worthy agencies or whether emphasis should be on projects of an exploratory or pioneering nature. This question, like many of the others that follow, may have been answered by the donor in his governing mandate. If not, the trustees in the course of making their decision probably will encounter the common claim that the major contributions of foundations flow from their freedom to supply "risk capital" for venturesome experiments and demonstrations. Many new ventures may not be undertaken by private enterprise if they offer no hope of profit or even of return of principal, by established philanthropic agencies for want of adequate resources, or by the government for fear of citizen disapproval of such use of tax money. It certainly has been true that foundation support has made possible many undertakings of benefit to mankind apparently without other potential sources of support. As a random illustration, the pioneering work of the Population Council with generous foundation support has been basic in the development of means for family limitation, particularly the oral contraceptive known as "the pill" and also the plastic intrauterine device, and in the growing acceptance in diverse parts of the world of the need for a rational balance of population and resources. If the subject of contraception is less frightening today to legislators, government administrators, and the public than it was earlier in the century, and if there is hope of meeting the crisis of the so-called population explosion without disaster, several foundations must be given credit for courageous pioneering grants. As another example, the extent to which the several social sciences now are able to serve the demands of government and industry, limited as they still may be, is directly related to foundation support in decades of public and government skepticism and hostility so strong that the social sciences could not be mentioned in the act creating the National Science Foundation in 1950. The list of grants for pioneering projects is long.

Yet no foundation should hesitate to concentrate its funds on projects of a more conservative nature. Relatively small foundations hardly may do otherwise with their limited resources. Consideration of pioneering proposals requires costly advice and investigation beyond the justifiable range of the great majority of foundations. Even large foundations properly may choose to make their grants to beneficiaries whose proposals and records are conservative rather than venturesome. Indeed, there is no large foundation that makes most of its grants for projects of an especially venturesome nature in the sense of pioneering or of challenging a highly regarded social value, as did the grants to the Population Council. This is not just a matter of trustee conservatism; it probably is even more a matter of what applicants want to do. The trustees' choice is limited to the question of whether or not to make some pioneering grants and, if so, in what proportion. Quite reasonably, the public which has given foundations the advantage of tax exemption and legal perpetuity, if desired, expects this to be the case and certainly would object if it were not.

There has been far too much emphasis on foundation funds as "venture capital" and consequent criticism of unexciting, passive grants. The actual choice facing trustees with sizable funds is not between glamorous ventures and somewhat routine allocations to worthy causes, but rather from three overlapping types of proposals that for convenience and somewhat arbitrarily may be categorized as essentially supportive, developmental, or innovative.

Under the classification "supportive" typically are grants for general ongoing activities to hospitals, churches, academic institutions, the Red Cross, museums, and other established tax-exempt agencies.

"Developmental" grants are those intended to improve or extend the activities already widely accepted as desirable of the same agencies that may receive supportive aid. Examples would be the foundation subsidy of the 200-inch telescope on Palomar Mountain, double the size of the previously largest telescope, the endowment of a new but otherwise not unique center for cancer research, or support for the expansion of a university.

"Innovative" grants are those hopefully designed to discover or demonstrate a better way of meeting a human need than presently is available, of taking practical advantage of new knowledge, of adapting to changed human circumstances. These may be called venturesome and some definitely have been venturesome; for example, the foundation grants for the development and greater use of contraceptives previously mentioned; the many early grants for Negro education and the improvement of race relations; the financing of the well-known and influential report on medical education by Abraham Flexner in the first decade of the present century. The bulk of innovative grants, however, have not been notably venturesome, although none the less praiseworthy on that account; for example, foundation-supported innovations in agricultural production in countries short of food such as Mexico, the Philippines, India, and others; the establishment of centers for research and instruction concerning foreign areas such as Russia, Southeast Asia, and other parts of the world; support of the American Law Institute for the production of an orderly restatement of the laws of the several states. The scattered illustrations of supportive, developmental, and innovative projects include grants to operating agencies and foundation operated projects. Similar illustrations could be provided of grants to individuals for support and expenses for study, research, and professional activities.[11]

No donor or trustee need feel embarrassed because his foundation devotes its funds to supportive proposals. Such support is essential for all types of social agencies and the need for such grants is much greater than the foundation money available. True, both the developmental and the innovative forms of philanthropy are excitingly appealing to many. True also, foundations are unique in their freedom and ability to foster exploratory and risky endeavors, but in practice these represent only by a small proportion of their allocations. Perspective has been distorted by the fact that the praiseworthy consequences of past developmental and innovative foundation investments have been well publicized and loom dramatically large in the eyes of the foundation community and the public. Donors and trustees, however, should realize that there are these three interrelated types of projects, which may be included in a foundation program with whatever differing degree of emphasis they choose, as permitted by mandate and resources. There is no logically compelling reason for the exclusion or inclusion of any one type. What is important is awareness of the differences in objectives, and de-

---

[11] For brief accounts of the contributions of foundations in the development of major fields of specialization, see the section on "Judgments Concerning the Value of Foundation Aid" in Warren Weaver, *U.S. Philanthropic Foundations: Their History, Structure, Management, and Record* (New York: Harper & Row, 1967), pp. 223–439.

cision on the basic, but not necessarily inviolable, policy of priorities concerning them.

The geographic scope of a foundation's interests may be limited to a local community, to a state or larger region of the country, to the United States as a whole, to a selected foreign country or area, or not at all. The small foundation usually is wise to restrict its activities to the local community where it has its headquarters and where its trustees reside. It then has the advantage of being managed by persons who either are familiar with local conditions or readily can learn what more they need to know. There is, of course, no reason that such local limitation should not be disregarded if some opportunity of exceptional interest outside the local area presents itself.

Pittsburgh, Pennsylvania, has benefited greatly from the programs of The A. W. Mellon Educational and Charitable Trust, Richard King Mellon Foundation, Sarah Mellon Scaife Foundation, Howard Heinz Endowment, The Buhl Foundation, The Pittsburgh Foundation, Pitcairn-Crabbe Foundation, Edgar J. Kaufmann Charitable Foundation, and Claude Worthington Benedum Foundation, all of which have concentrated expenditures in the Pittsburgh area and with a remarkable degree of informal but effective mutual understanding and cooperation. The Kansas City Association of Trusts and Foundations, an agency that "assists four separate foundations in the development of coordinated programs of grants-in-aid to worthy community undertakings," offers another example of philanthropic effectiveness at the local community level. These illustrations have been chosen from innumerable possibilities because they are examples of exceptional cooperation among foundations with consequent exceptional advantage to their communities. Inter-foundation community-wide planning and cooperation is rare in comparison with the practice of considering applications and making grants as independent one-by-one decisions, a major weakness in the practice of small foundations with mainly local concern.

Foundations restricting themselves to particular states are not unusual; for example, the Rosenberg Foundation is active only in California, the Clayton Fund and the Moody Foundation only in Texas. The Louis W. and Maud Hill Family Foundation operates a program with broad interests geographically restricted mainly to the upper midwestern and the northwestern parts of the United States. Unless the state or region is thinly populated and somewhat distinctive in character, as might be said of Utah or the distressed area of Appalachia, its philanthropic needs almost certainly are too diverse and the area too large to be intensively familiar to a foundation's management. Otherwise, whatever justification there may have been in the past for the selection of such large geographic areas of operation rather than the country as a whole has been dissipated by nationwide economic and cultural integration. The argument sometimes still heard that it is fitting for a man to devote his philanthropic funds to the place where they were accumulated is based on the false premise that the economic source of a fortune is the geographic location of a business, a premise that requires the further false assumption that there are economically self-contained districts in the United States. One may appreciate the sentimental desire of a donor to favor that part of the country with which he identifies himself and his financial success and at the same time recognize its philanthropic illogicality. Practicality as well as logic supports the view that the rational choice is between a local community and no less than the entire nation.

Most foundations are limited by mandate or in practice to the support of activities within the United States. There is, however, no reason in law, tradition, or the basic principles of philanthropy for doing so, but there are some Internal Revenue Service restrictions. Although an individual will not receive tax exemption for his direct philanthropic gifts to causes in other countries, foundations are under no similar legal restraint. Philanthropy across national boundaries has a long tradition in the United States that begins with charitable gifts from Europe to America. There is an early reverse precedent for international philanthropy in a shipment in 1676 of food purchased by the Protestants of Dublin to colonists in need as a consequence of King Philip's War.[12] The contributions from overseas to American intellectual

---

[12] Merle Curti, *American Philanthropy Abroad: A History* (New Brunswick, N.J.: Rutgers University Press, 1963), p. 3. Dr. Curti's volume is recommended in its entirety as the single full and well-balanced account of American contributions to health, welfare, and education in other countries.

life of James Smithson and Cecil Rhodes are well known. From earliest times Americans as individuals have responded generously with aid to the distress needs following disaster in other parts of the world. Foundations also respond with funds for relief to disasters abroad, but because of their unique capability for long-term planning and continuing programs they are more distinguished for their support of not just temporary ameliorative aid but particularly of innovating constructive programs.

The deed of trust that in 1909 was the actual origin of The Rockefeller Foundation stipulated that the funds then donated were to be used "to promote the well-being and to advance the civilization of the peoples of the United States and its territories and possessions and of foreign lands in the acquisition and dissemination of knowledge, in the prevention and relief of suffering, and in the promotion of any and all of the elements of human progress."[13] A better statement of philanthropic purpose is hardly imaginable. This mandated concern with the well-being of all mankind led the way not only for other internationally oriented foundations, but through the demonstrations offered by subsequent overseas activities may also be claimed to have prepared the way for more recent governmental aid in other countries. The worldwide achievements of The Rockefeller Foundation in the fields of health, education, and agriculture certainly provided encouragement and guidance for others who have accepted the concept of the unity of mankind and recognized the reality of world interdependence. Of course, there still are those who argue that charity should begin and end at home. The trouble with their argument, apart from its inhumanity, is that there is no home in the United States uninfluenced by lack of well-being abroad.

A word of caution for foundations contemplating overseas programs is in order, however. It is no simple task to attempt good works in foreign countries, each with its own cherished ways of life and its own standards of proper behavior. These frequently are at odds with our own ways and standards. Furthermore, like us, they will not enjoy, although in time of great need

---

[13] Robert Shaplen, *Toward the Well-Being of Mankind* (Garden City, N.Y.: Doubleday & Co., Inc., 1964), p. 6.

they may accept, having things done for them by outsiders. The basic and essential rules of procedure are that other peoples must not be overwhelmed, and they must always participate as full partners in any venture intended for their benefit and even be encouraged to do it alone the way that seems best to them. The approval and cooperation of the concerned governments, of the relevant health, welfare, educational, economic, and other agencies and their personnel, and of the public, is crucial. Naturally, advanced technical knowledge and practical skills, as in medicine, agriculture, and engineering, need to be made available, but as unobtrusively as possible and through their accepted channels and agencies. This requires thorough familiarity with their language, their culture, and their social structure. Unless an American foundation is willing and able to take fully into account the differing characteristics and sensitivities of the people and government of another country and freely share the selection of goals and the direction of operations, the proper place for its charity is, indeed, at home.

Many foundations refuse to consider, or give low priority to, requests for funds for buildings, endowment, general operating expenses, or deficit reimbursement. Where such a policy prevails and is challenged by an agency in need of aid for one or more of these purposes, the response is likely to be that these are among the less effective forms of philanthropy for a foundation, particularly for a foundation whose trustees accept the view that they have unique capability, opportunity, and responsibility for more exploratory and innovative investment. For many it is neither venturesome nor an exceptionally stimulating source of satisfaction to contribute to construction costs, to a capital fund, to ongoing activity expenses, or to the payment of a debt. That there are two sides to such debate is evidenced by the fact that many foundations do spend large portions of their funds, and often all of them, for one or more of these four purposes. There even is one foundation that announces that it is particularly interested in making grants to meet deficits.

Obviously many institutions such as hospitals, colleges and universities, museums, and others, particularly those offering continuing services to large numbers of people, must have their own buildings. Only those requiring relatively small housing space can efficiently avoid the costs of building ownership and maintenance and the drain on staff time of real estate management by renting. Those that must have their own quarters are up against the fact that time and social change make previously adequate housing obsolete and may require expansion to meet the needs of a growing population to serve. Foundations that regard bricks and mortar as a poor investment sometimes do so on the ground that not only are they obligated to be more innovative, but also that buildings can be otherwise financed. Buildings do have a strong appeal to wealthy individuals in the satisfaction afforded by lasting identification with a substantial structure. It also frequently is possible to finance a new building by borrowing against future income. In some instances, such as college dormitories, they may even be made to pay for themselves, wholly or in large part. Federal funds also have been available for some building costs, particularly hospitals and university buildings. Yet no one argues that such sources are meeting all necessary building costs of charitable and educational institutions. Nor can it be argued that innovation in philanthropic endeavor is independent of housing facilities. The decision to include or exclude grants for buildings can only be made on the basis of the individual foundation's resources, objectives, and preferences. If they are included in a foundation's program, the question of a supplementary grant for maintenance should be considered, as it often is not. The upkeep on a new building can be a serious drain on an institution's resources.

Endowment grants, like grants for construction, are included in the programs of some foundations and excluded in the case of others. Policy excluding grants for endowment, however, is more likely to be based frankly on the size of allocations required to provide an income adequate for immediate significant activity. The income from an endowment of half a million dollars, for example, no longer is adequate to meet the salary and fringe benefits of a professor at a major university, to say nothing of the costs of office space, secretarial help, and other attendant items of expense. The same amount of money could be generous for a significant research project or some other immediate university need. Furthermore, endowment requires great confidence in the continuation of the need for which it was given and in the

future effectiveness of the agency to which it is given, both ordinarily matters of some doubt in a time of rapid social change,
including change in the value of the dollar. The reluctance of
many trustees concerning endowment grants also seems to be
related to the fact that there is more satisfaction ordinarily to be
gained in direct involvement in a current project than in contributing to the capital funds of another agency, an action akin
to a delegation of responsibility. On the other hand, institutions
do need the stability provided by a reasonable capital sum. It is
desirable, however, that this capital sum not be so rigidly restricted that its use cannot be adapted to unanticipated social
change. Such an unfortunate contingency may be easily guarded
against by providing at the time of gift that after the lapse of
some period of time, possibly ten or fifteen years, depending on
one's estimate of the potential rapidity of social change, the purpose for which it was made be modified by some procedure simpler than *cy pres* court action, and that the principal as well as
the income may be expended in the discretion of the recipient.
Even though foundations themselves legally may have perpetual
life, it is unrealistic to believe that any group of trustees can predict specific social needs or their dollar requirements beyond a
decade or so.

There is again a division of opinion among foundations in
policy and practice concerning grants for expenses for general
administration and services. Those that do not make such grants,
or do so only reluctantly and in exceptional cases, are severely
criticized by many persons engaged directly in supplying charitable and educational services at the working level in the very
fields of interest to the foundations at the developmental and
innovative levels. Universities complain that foundations support
special projects and developments, but not their basic ongoing
educational work. Hospitals lament that foundations are more
concerned with medical research than with the care of the sick.
Welfare agencies are distressed that foundations spend their
money for studying crime, poverty, family problems, and individual inadequacy, but offer little for the relief of those in trouble.
Taking foundations as a whole, these charges, of course, are
false, for most foundations, particularly the family foundations,
give most of their money for direct aid to individuals in need

served by established agencies. Only a comparatively small number of foundations, mostly the larger and older ones, have developed policies that focus on the advancement of knowledge and innovative projects for their potential contributions to the improvement of practice and the development of preventive measures. The fact that they are large and well known makes them easy but unrepresentative targets.

Few as they are in number, foundations that are convinced that grants for ongoing operating costs do not offer the best opportunities for the use of their funds do have a numerically disproportionate share of foundation funds. They have been and are influential beyond the proportion of their number and even of their dollars in the development of philanthropic standards and practices. They are not unmindful of immediate ameliorative needs, but justify their less direct and future-oriented programs in terms of the need for basic social advance and by the fact that their resources would constitute a relatively insignificant fraction of present direct philanthropic aid requirements and expenditures if totally so devoted. In the early 1960's foundation expenditures amounted to about 7 per cent of all private giving. The percentage devoted to developmental and innovative projects, of course, was much smaller. Eighty per cent came from individuals, the rest from bequests, corporation gifts, and the endowment earnings of tax-exempt institutions. The total of private philanthropy was about eleven or twelve billion dollars per year.[14] When the billions of dollars spent for health, education, welfare, and cultural activities by the federal, state, and local governments of the United States are added, the comparatively very minor possible foundation contribution to the direct support of the activities of operating agencies is evident. As F. Emerson Andrews has put it: "Many foundations have accepted the doctrine that their limited funds should be used chiefly as the venture capital of philanthropy, to be spent in enterprises requiring risk and foresight, not likely to be supported by government or private individuals. In their fields of special interest

---

[14] The estimates of private philanthropic giving in the early 1960's are taken from Ralph L. Nelson, *The Investment Policies of Foundations* (New York: Russell Sage Foundation, 1967), pp. 6–7.

they prefer to aid research, designed to push forward the frontiers of knowledge, or pilot demonstrations, resulting in improved procedures apt to be widely copied."[15] This is by no means a categorical criticism of the literally thousands of foundations that do devote their funds to direct and immediate aid. If they are comparatively small, it is extremely difficult for them to do anything else wisely. Furthermore, there is no shortage of inadequacies and gaps in both government and private programs for direct aid that offer exceptional opportunities for supplementary foundation grants.

Thus far it has been assumed that foundation expenditures will be made as grants to somewhat fortuitous applicants. This is not true for all foundations, but more often is the case than is desirable for effective operation. If a foundation has clear and definite objectives, it need not be left to chance mail and visitors to bring in hopefully suitable proposals. There is no reason other than unnecessary fear of premature commitment for not initiating discussion with an individual or agency concerning mutual interests and encouraging an application if it is found that there are a desire, capability, and need for support of an activity in accord with a foundation's program. Often a fortuitous application unsuitable in the form submitted may suggest that it could be revised after consultation to be in accord with the recipient foundation's objectives without subverting the applicant's purpose. There is, of course, always a danger that proposals may be tailored unjustifiably to what is understood to be a foundation's preference. Naturally, care must be taken both in initiating proposals and in suggesting proposal revisions to avoid enticing applications for which there is inferior competence or no better than secondary interest. Nevertheless, without the exercise of some foundation initiative there is a good chance that a foundation's objectives will be approached in an unnecessarily random fashion through limitation of consideration to applications that just happen to come in.

On occasion a foundation's objective may be blocked by the unavailability of a suitable operating agency. A new agency some-

---

[15] F. Emerson Andrews, "Introduction," in Marianna O. Lewis, editor, *The Foundation Directory, Edition 3*, previously cited, p. 50.

times may be created under such circumstances. Quite a number of important organizations today owe their existence, if not exclusively to foundation iintiative, at least to initial foundation cooperative planning and support. Some such bodies have been created for a specific task to be completed in a few years, after which they are dissolved by prearrangement, as in the case of the East European Fund which was initiated and supported by The Ford Foundation. Others have been designed for longer life: for example, the Fund for the Republic and the Center for Advanced Study in Behavioral Sciences, both also with Ford Foundation initiative and support.

It is rarely if ever true that a foundation may be given total credit or blame for the creation of such agencies, for there must be some independent individuals with prior interest in the objective in question, involved in the act of creation and later willing to undertake operations. It is fair to say, however, that in numerous instances a foundation has been a necessary if not a sufficient initiating factor. There is no reason that a foundation should not participate to any degree necessary in the creation of a new organization that will further its objectives, provided that the need is real, that qualified personnel is eager to cooperate, and that responsibility for financing is accepted until such time as the organization becomes self-supporting or its orderly termination is indicated.

The greatest degree of foundation initiative is to be found in the actual operation of a project or program of its own. Of course, if this is done exclusively it may be said that a foundation has given up its character as a foundation and become an institute or other kind of operating agency. Actually, the foundations generally referred to as operating foundations are only so in part and also make at least a few grants to other agencies or independent individuals. This has been true, for example, of Russell Sage Foundation, the Twentieth Century Fund, and the Milbank Memorial Fund. Whatever the operating program of a foundation, it is practically inevitable that some particular important segments will be found to be more advantageously financed by grants for work by individuals associated with a university or other agency and unable or unwilling to join the foundation staff even on a temporary basis. Furthermore, some other agency on occasion will have better facilities for carrying out a part of the foundation's program than the foundation itself. The unfortunate alternatives to taking advantage of such external opportunities would be to leave an unnecessary gap in the program or to bring in an inferior person. By definition and in practice, there is no such thing as an exclusively operating foundation, only a difference in the relative amounts of money spent in direct operation and by grants.

It is not unusual for foundations that spend most of their money in the form of grants also to engage in direct operations. The Rockefeller Foundation is well known for its operating achievements in the fields of health and agriculture. Carnegie Corporation of New York itself conducted the study of the American Negro, which resulted in the publication of *An American Dilemma* by Gunnar Myrdal, with the assistance of Richard Sterner and Arnold Rose. The Danforth Foundation, which describes itself as both an operating and a grant-making foundation, spent a little over $2.6 million in grants and a little under the same amount on its operating program in the fiscal year ending June 30, 1965. Whether or not a primarily grant-making foundation should engage in direct operations is no more than a matter of its own judgment concerning its capability in comparison with the capability of other available auspices. There is a likely by-product gain from direct foundation operation in that it affords opportunity for the staff, and to some extent for the trustees, for realistic contact with the problems and working conditions faced by grantees and helps to reduce a tendency to estrangement from actual as well as potential beneficiaries consequent to isolated administration.

Not infrequently a foundation favorably impressed by an application will want to consider whether to make an outright contribution or to offer partial support on condition that some specified sum be raised elsewhere within a definite subsequent time. This type of provisional grant long has been known as a "matching grant," but in recent years has acquired the designation of "challenge grant," possibly in part because it does present a money-raising challenge, but also no doubt because it sounds somewhat less dictatorial. The euphemism, however, does not change the fact that such grants do put heavy pressure on the potential recipient to raise more money and also on other foundations and individuals to contribute at least in part for a reason not related to their judgment of worth. Such partial support may be merely a consequence of limited funds, with the matching provision added as a stimulus for extra effort to obtain the total needed.

The basic argument for matching grants, however, is that reliance on a single source of support under some circumstances may be unfortunate for longer term financing of an agency. A broad range of foundations and individuals with financial interest certainly is to be desired by any agency. The term "matching," incidentally, is misleading in that it suggests equality in amounts, for it is not unusual to require that two or three or even more times the amount of a matching grant be obtained from other sources. A foundation making a matching grant may expect to be told that the condition is very much appreciated because of its anticipated helpfulness in raising additional funds. Quite often the expression of appreciation will be entirely sincere, but also quite often there will be unexpressed resentment because of the compulsive element and the fact that the partial support offered would be most useful in itself regardless of whether the total of the matching requirement or only some portion of it was raised later.

Matching grants have been a fund-expanding foundation device since the first decade of the present century. In recent years the federal government has adopted the same technique for exerting pressure on foundations by offering similar conditional grants in great number through such agencies as the National Foundation on the Arts and Humanities, the Office of Education, and the Office of Economic Opportunity. Frederick deW. Bolman of the Esso Education Foundation has pointed out three basic considerations to be kept in mind by a foundation before yielding too generously to such invitations: "First, matching grants are justified only on the basis of promise or ability to provide private dollars, and this should not be the thrust of government dollars. Second, activity far beyond the arena of public approval should be the primary work of private foundations. And third, Federal matching grants if responded to widely spell the death of the real work of private foundations as we have known it."[16] Matching grants even in moderation may have irritating and unfortunate results, but in the excess permitted by the enormous resources of the federal government they can be a major threat to the innovating role of private philanthropy.

The token grant may be considered a sort of distant relative of the matching grant. Applications for comparatively small sums sometimes are made to obtain the helpful prestige of a foundation grant for use in other solicitations more than for the money requested. These are not always easy to detect and there is some likelihood that favorable action may be unduly influenced by their small size. There is no basic objection to a foundation's lending of its name, particularly when it is able financially to do little more, provided that it does so with care and would do more if it could. All foundation grants are in fact a certification of judgment of worth that should not be given merely out of good will or because little money is involved.

A distinctive form of matching grant, also not necessarily in equal amounts, is agreement by two or more foundations to join in supporting a proposal of common interest. This may be a consequence of the fact that a foundation just does not have the money available to go it alone on some project before it, although otherwise it would be glad to do so. Another strong reason for inter-foundation cooperation is that there are some projects that clearly should not be supported by a single foundation. For example, when Russell Sage Foundation was convinced that there should be a center where all information obtainable about foundations would be available to all comers, it found that its own funds were inadequate for the task. Carnegie Corporation of New York, on being asked if it was interested in the idea, responded by making the initial grant that in 1956 established The Foundation Library Center, renamed The Foundation Center late in 1968. It was later joined in its support by The Ford Foundation, The Rockefeller Foundation, W. K. Kellogg Foundation, Russell Sage Foundation, Alfred P. Sloan Foundation, The Danforth

---

[16] Frederick deW. Bolman, "Caution Needed in Matching Grants," *Foundation News*, vol. 8, January, 1967, p. 6.

Foundation, The William H. Donner Foundation, Charles F. Kettering Foundation, and Richard King Mellon Foundation. Support by a number of foundations, of course, also has the advantage of reducing the chance of a financial crisis should one withdraw as a result of change in policy or some other circumstance.

It has been said that a small foundation should not put all of its eggs in one or two baskets and that a large one should stay out of the retail business. Neither metaphor offers firm guidance for trustees. There is no reason that a small foundation should not devote all of its funds to the work of one or two agencies. Indeed, there are circumstances when it could be wise to go to the extreme of reserving all income for a number of years for a single project, perhaps for a new wing for a hospital or a laboratory for a university, as may be done in spite of the rule against unreasonable accumulations provided that the approval of the Internal Revenue Service is obtained. A large foundation, in turn, may make many advantageous small grants, perhaps for fellowships, research projects, or creative work in the arts and humanities. The John Simon Guggenheim Memorial Foundation, with assets of over $60 million, spends all of its money for comparatively small fellowships. A grant of only $1,227 by The Rockefeller Foundation for laboratory equipment was of significant help to Howard W. Florey and Ernst Chain in the purification of penicillin. A better understanding of the uses of large grants can follow from direct involvement with individuals and agencies working on small-scale projects. There is some truth in the overstatement that a $5,000 grant requires more time and care than one of $500,000, but the trouble can be well worthwhile in the realistic perspective to be gained by keeping in touch with lesser models of the beneficiaries of large grants, not just with representatives of intermediate operating or channeling agencies.

Grants may be made either to institutions or to individuals. Many grants to institutions, however, actually are for the use of specified individuals for specified purposes. The institution under such circumstances is in fact primarily a fiscal agent with varying supervisory responsibility, depending on the terms of the grant. Dependence on institutional oversight of work on a grant with a named individual in charge may be risky, for all too frequently the institution may do little or nothing beyond relying on the competence and integrity of the project director. Such negligence may be criticized, but it is natural, often even inevitable, because more often than not the individual in charge knows more than anyone else in the institution about the subject of his work and no institution wants to be accused of undue interference with the freedom of its professional staff, especially in research and innovative tasks.

A troublesome question in institutional grants is the determination of the amount, if any, that should be included for "overhead" costs of a project. Grants for innovative or expanded programs can be a serious drain on basic funds and staff time justifying financial recompense. Special projects conducted by staff members (academic personnel) or by institutional subunits (research centers or medical clinics) usually involve indirect and partially hidden costs, as for space and its upkeep, and for fiscal and other administrative obligations. A grant for a needed new building can be ruinous if without a supplementary allocation for maintenance. A complicating factor has been the adventitious influence of the varying and sometimes generous (at least in comparison with foundation practice) allowance for indirect costs provided by government grants to, and contracts with, tax-exempt institutions in recent years. There is no reliable rule of thumb for deciding when or how much to allow for indirect costs. It may be reasonable to allocate anything from zero to some indefinite maximum, perhaps as high as 100 per cent, of the basic grant. If a grant is for ongoing normal activities, there obviously is no "overhead" cost. At the other extreme, if a foundation suggests a project because of some special interest of its own in which an institution, although qualified and willing, has no particular interest, a service is being purchased and a price well above indirect costs justifiably may be paid. Between the extremes, all that can be done is to estimate indirect costs without forgetting.that some of them are well concealed and all are only roughly measurable in dollars.

Institutional grants do have important advantages and are the most common form of allocation. These advantages include the avoidance of project management and concern with fiscal details, a reduction, but not elimination, of responsibility for evaluation, the opportunity for large grants rather than "scatteration giving," and help in counteracting any tendency toward narrow perspective through the diversity of contacts and outlets afforded. Although most foundation grants are for projects under institutional auspices, with fellowships being the main but still minor exception, in fact success or failure always depends on the individuals involved. The personnel to be engaged in an institutional project under foundation consideration need to be given no less scrutiny than the project design.

A few miscellaneous generalizations about foundations' practice may be mentioned most briefly. There is no serious dispute about them in the abstract, but they often fail of consideration in trustee action.

An application supported primarily by a demonstration of financial need rather than by a full and clear statement of procedure for accomplishing an objective at most should be tabled pending adequate operational information. It is common for an agency, confident that its worth is self-evident, to request support without presenting much more than evidence of financial distress.

If a proposal is designed to effect a major change within an institution or community, the chances of success must be judged slight unless there is strong and responsible supporting leadership within the setting. Room for institutional or community improvement is limitless, but change for the better usually requires wise and strong effort from within the agency or area.

Current popularity of a philanthropic field should not be allowed to distort a foundation's program. There are surges and recessions of interest, in plain words, fads and fashions, in research, education, health care, cultural affairs, international relations, and all other areas of philanthropic concern, that tend unduly to influence foundation action. On the other hand, duplication in areas of foundation activity is not to be avoided on that ground alone, for multiple attack in reasonable degree usually is advantageous.

Prompt action on requests is not only a courtesy, but also a recognition that frequently applicants are under severe pressure of time. Board meetings for action on proposals once a year may serve trustees' convenience, but they can be badly out of phase with the schedules of potential beneficiaries imposed by the nature of their work.

No useful purpose is served by attempting a detailed explanation to an unsuccessful applicant of precisely why his proposal was declined unless the reason was purely technical, for example, "out of program." It does no good to tell a rejected applicant that his subject was regarded as relatively unimportant, his project design poor, or that he was thought incompetent for the proposed task. Furthermore, there frequently is no simple reason for rejection, for individual trustees may be negative for quite different reasons, usually unrecorded.

Relations with Grantees: Restraints and Evaluation

Although foundations generally claim and believe that their responsibility ends when a grant has been made, except to be reasonably alert for gross violations of the terms of a grant, in fact it is most difficult, if not impossible, for trustees to be unconcerned about the effectiveness with which grants are used. A few foundations are able and willing to help a recipient agency or individual in the development of a project if help is needed, a need not uncommon in the case of innovating projects. Whether or not foundation help can be given, foundations need to know how effective their grants have been both for the further development of their own programs and for guidance in case there are subsequent applications by earlier grantees, as is very likely.

The question of the proper concern of a foundation in a project after a grant has been made is debated too often as though there were only the alternatives of strict laissez-faire, except for a more or less full report on expenditures and accomplishments, or of such close supervision that it amounts to domination. Neither extreme may be well defended, although there are foundations practicing as fully as possible one or the other of the extremes. The phrase "as fully as possible" is included because trustees, on the one hand, may hardly be totally unconcerned with the use of their grants nor, on the other, are there many beneficiaries who are willing to be entirely subservient. As has been said earlier, foundations do not give away money as one gives a birthday present or small change to a panhandler. Their grants are in fact a purchase, albeit a purchase for the benefit of others. It follows that there is a responsibility for assurance that the goods were delivered as purchased. It does not follow that the purchaser should interfere in the process of delivery, although he may provide aid if needed and if he has the skill to do so. At a minimum, he should have the skill to evaluate the results of his investment. For this small foundations must rely either on the services of trustees or on properly qualified consultants employed ad hoc or on a more general continuing basis. The larger foundations also may make use of their trustees and of consultants, but the task is likely to be so complicated and burdensome that full-time staff will be found preferable. More will be said later about foundation staff and its functions. Here it is emphasized that one basic staff function is post-grant evaluation and that a possible additional function is consultative assistance to beneficiaries in the course of their work.[17]

In all a foundation's relations with others there should be strict regard for the individual's right to privacy. This has been defined as "the right of the individual to decide for himself how much he will share with others his thoughts, his feelings, and the facts of his personal life."[18] It is a matter of concern to foundations both because of the confidential nature of many of their communications and because of the nature of a number of projects they support.

The confidential nature of applications submitted to foundations, of the supporting documents and referees' reports, and of trustee discussions and negative actions is well recognized and observed. Foundations are public trusts and their basic activities should be made known to the public. These are reported in abstract to the Internal Revenue Service on Form 990-A and are available to any interested person. Many foundations also publish periodic reports and distribute them widely. Their negative ac-

---

[17] For further discussion of foundation-grantee relations, see Leonard S. Cottrell, Jr., "Effective Relations Between Foundations and Grantees," in Henry Sellin, editor, *Proceedings of the Sixth Biennial Conference on Charitable Foundations*, New York University (Albany, N.Y.: Matthew Bender & Co., Inc., 1963), pp. 37–52.

[18] Executive Office of the President, Office of Science and Technology, *Privacy and Behavioral Research* (Washington: Government Printing Office, 1967), p. 2.

tions, however, are kept confidential for the compelling reason that they could unnecessarily damage the reputations of unsuccessful applicants if publicized. Appraisals of individual and institutional proposals also are kept confidential, whether favorable or otherwise, for obvious and sufficient reasons. Violations of the confidential aspects of foundation transactions and records are rare. Such matters properly are considered to be strictly private.

The other aspect of privacy with which many foundations should be concerned is the possible invasion of personal privacy in the conduct of projects which they support. The right of privacy as previously defined often has been invaded by foundation projects in medical research and care, in research in the behavioral sciences such as anthropology, sociology, and psychology, and in social work. Some invasion of individual privacy in such areas is necessary and unavoidable both for the advancement of knowledge crucial in human affairs and in some cases for the service of individual needs. It cannot be argued, however, that individual privacy should be invaded in research or professional practice without the informed consent of the subject of research, patient or client, without adequate safeguards against physical and psychological damage, and without absolute guarantees of confidentiality. The problem of balancing the potential gain to society from the knowledge hopefully to be gained or the possible advantage to the individual in need of professional service against the costs of privacy invasion is not a simple one and has no categorical resolution.[19] All that can be said is that foundation trustees and staff need to be sensitive to the privacy rights of the intended subjects in any project under consideration as balanced against competing individual and social needs.

Sources of Information and Advice. The philanthropic value of a foundation's expenditures bears no necessary direct relation to the number of dollars involved, but must be measured by the

---

[19] For pioneering discussion of the issues involved, see: Alan F. Westin, *Privacy and Freedom* (New York: Atheneum Publishers, 1967); Oscar M. Ruebhausen and Orville G. Brim, Jr., "Privacy and Behavioral Research," in Harry W. Jones, editor, *Law and the Social Role of Science* (New York: The Rockefeller University Press, 1966), pp. 80–105.

wisdom with which they were expended. One could scarcely disagree with the statement made in 1934 by Frederick P. Keppel,
then president of Carnegie Corporation of New York, that money
"is always secondary in importance to the idea and the worker."[20]
The selection of the most promising ideas from the many offered
and of workers qualified for their development is both the prime
and the most difficult task of foundation trustees.

The privilege of utilizing the advantages of a foundation for
philanthropic purposes carries with it the obligation, the social
duty, of informed and effective allocation of foundation funds.
Family foundations commonly depend for their effectiveness in
accomplishing the foundation's purpose solely on the knowledge
and wisdom of the trustees, or even of the donor himself, through
trustee default as a matter of courtesy to him. The trustee attitude that, after all, it is "his money" is very common, although in
law and fact it no longer is his. Acquiescence in this form of
conduit foundation operation is understandable, although legally
indefensible. Extension of such domination to other members of
the donor's family, his children and grandchildren, is not rare.
It is highly questionable as a matter of social policy. For these
descendants, it never was "their money" any more than a gift by
a relative or forebear to a university, church, or operating charity
would give a descendant any special claim on the funds.

As observed earlier, donor domination of foundation grants can
work well with local allocations where beneficiaries are well
known and with allocations to "blue chip" organizations such as
community chests or academic institutions. In such instances a
foundation's selective procedure is practically identical with that
of personal philanthropic donations. However, a foundation unwilling to limit its benefactions to well-known local and "blue
chip" organizations is in need of more investigative and evalua-
tive aid than ordinarily can be provded by the donor and trustees.
Knowledgeable and impartial consultants or staff, or both, are
required as sources of relevant information.

Consultants need to be chosen not only on the basis of their
knowledge of the field in which proposals fall, but also with re-

---

[20] Frederick P. Keppel, *Philanthropy and Learning* (New York: Columbia
University Press, 1936), p. 4.

gard for their objectivity. There is no field of foundation activity in which there are not plenty of experts who are persuasively biased in favor of or against particular institutions or schools of thought within their specialty. Ad hoc or continuing consultants work very well if well chosen as aids to trustees in reaching decisions regarding the worth and feasibility of proposals, and the suitability of the institutions and personnel involved. It is important that they be used as aids and not as arbiters. Consultants may occasionally find themselves, unwittingly, being used by partisans in a dispute among trustees (or staff) over questions of policy. It is a most precarious position for the consultant, and a sure tip-off that the responsible authorities have failed to achieve the collegial principle appropriate to their deliberations. A fee for genuine consulting service is proper and desirable, but many specialists will give aid happily without compensation as an obligation of their profession. Consultants are used extensively by large foundations to supply expert advice not within the competence of the staff. They are of especial advantage to the smaller foundation whose limited resources and program do not justify the cost of continuing staff. In the case of one medium-sized and long-established foundation, the Milbank Memorial Fund, technical consultation is in part formally established. In addition to the Board of Directors, whose members are in effect trustees, there is a Technical Board concerned primarily with the Fund's interests in medical research. The Fund also supports research and action programs in demography and public health, fields not represented on the Technical Board. Two members of the Technical Board also serve as directors.

Policy decisions are the responsibility of the board of trustees, but in a large foundation operating in one or more professionalized fields full-time staff aid is needed to supply basic facts, present debatable issues, and suggest the probable consequences of possible alternative choices. The general principle holds that policies are decided by the trustees and that the staff assists as directed in their activities. Actually in a large and well-staffed foundation these functions merge in some degree, depending on the qualities of the trustees and staff, the extent of professionalization of the area of activity, and the nature of a particular policy issue. Nevertheless, the trustees cannot avoid their responsibility for foundation actions by hand-washing delegation of any of their duties to staff.

If a foundation is able to afford full-time staff aid, there is a choice between the employment of persons professionally knowledgeable in the areas of activity and lay administrators with suitable qualities of a more general nature. Both kinds of foundation staff have made distinguished records. The lay administrator is likely to be somewhat less influential in trustee decisions, for, as one has remarked, his presentation of issues and proposals to the board must be made with no more backing of expertise than that possessed by anyone else present. Yet the previously quoted former president of Carnegie Corporation, Frederick P. Keppel, without question was extraordinarily effective in guiding that foundation's program although not professionally trained in its areas of activity. Examples of lay foundation administrators with somewhat routine accomplishments, no doubt because the trustees wished it so, are nevertheless far more common. The trustees' decision concerning the desirability of highly qualified professional staff should only be based on their concept of the staff services that will be most helpful in achieving the foundation's objectives, not on any hard and fast operating principle. It may be in point, however, to observe that in recent years the foundations best known for their philanthropic achievements increasingly have been staffed by men distinguished by relevant professional competence.

If more than two or three high-level staff members are employed, there is a choice in organization between the university or a more strictly hierarchical pattern. In the former, function and authority within a specialized area are closely related, with the administrative officers ideally concerned with the more general aspects of operation. In the latter, the chain of command is all-inclusive and omnipresent. The weakness in the all-encompassing hierarchical pattern is that it is most difficult to secure the services of superior personnel down the line, with the result that the staff is likely to be made up mainly of *de facto* messenger boys unable to talk with applicants on their level, represent the foundation with confidence in negotiations concerning proposals, or contribute much to program development. It is not mere coincidence that universities are able to retain the services of distinguished professors and flourish regardless of the academic distinction of their presidents and deans. Each professor has an area of functional autonomy; he is king in his own domain.

One other university pattern also can be helpful in securing and retaining superior staff. As universities permit and stimulate teaching staff to advance their careers as specialists through research and professional practice, may not foundations make similar provision in suitable instances both to make employment more attractive and to enable staff to keep up with their fields and thereby serve the foundation more efficiently? This has been a strength of the so-called operating foundations, and is an argument for the direct undertaking of some projects by the predominantly grant-making foundation. But there is no reason that any foundation should not offer staff free time, and even support, for independent professional activity.

The list of possible staff services, in addition to mere housekeeping duties, is long. Two already have been mentioned in another connection, the evaluation of accomplishments by beneficiaries and assistance to grantees in the course of their work if needed. Practically all proposals require checking, supplementary information, and review prior to presentation for board decision. Many, probably most, will be found unsuitable in terms of quality, available resources, or foundation policy. These either may be winnowed out by the staff with no more than a brief report to the trustees on what was done, or, if there are not too many in terms of trustee time available, presented for board action with short explanations of the staff's negative recommendations. However, a proposal should be presented in full if there is any reason whatever for believing that even a single trustee might question a staff judgment of unsuitability or suggest a departure from established policy. A foundation administrator who is so selective in the proposals brought to his trustees for action that rejections are rare or do not occur probably has accepted excessive responsibility, no matter how much confidence the board may have in him. It is very unlikely that the staff will not receive borderline applications. Furthermore, a board that sees only applications definitely deserving approval can lose interest, developing a possibly correct sense that it is serving as a rubber stamp.

As has been emphasized, policy determination is a trustee function that may not be delegated. Yet in professionalized areas of activity policy decision may not safely be left for decision by a board acting solely on the background of relevant knowledge that happens to be in the possession of its members. Similarly, the choice of a field of activity and program planning requires more than casual information about the relative philanthropic opportunities of alternatives. Also, a board of trustees with only layman knowledge of a field of venturesome operation may not rely with confidence on applicants' supporting documents and the comments of others who happen to come to mind as possible sources of good advice. The foundation that accepts developmental or innovating and not only rather routine supportive proposals consequently is in need of staff capable of serving as intermediary between applicants with professional sophistication and its lay trustees.

Foundations have been charged both with wasting money on staff and also with improperly delegating authority to employees. So far as wasting money is concerned, that depends on the quality of the staff in relation to a foundation's objectives. The optimum size of staff is less related to a foundation's financial resources than to what it is trying to do. The percentage of total expenditures chargeable to overhead may only be judged foundation by foundation in relation to program and operating effectiveness. Trustees and staff have a tendency to be overly timid about administrative expenditures and take pride when they are very low, although in fact their parsimony may deserve criticism.

Delegation of authority in the larger foundations is unavoidable and proper, both legally and ethically, although no doubt there have been instances where it has been carried to unreasonable and blameworthy extremes. What may not be delegated is responsibility. Trustees must decide issues concerning financial and program policy and act directly on at least the larger appropriations if not on all.

It is rather common for trustees to accord to the staff authority to make small grants that clearly are in accord with an explicit program objective or are desirable for exploratory purposes in relation to program planning. This may be done either by setting a maximum sum for any staff allocation or by setting aside a relatively small fund for expenditure in the discretion of the staff for payment of consultants, for support of small projects within the foundation program, and for outside aid in program planning and development. There is every reason also to delegate to the staff the authority to decline proposals clearly out of program or of obviously poor quality, preferably with a subsequent report to the board for its information about the total range of requests. Such informational reports to the trustees also protect the staff against speculative criticism that rejection has been improper.

If a foundation does employ staff charged with more than housekeeping and errand-boy duties, the widely accepted corporation management principle that authority and function belong together requires recognition. The scope and limits of both need to be definitely understood and followed as applied not only to staff, but also to trustees. Of course, there will be some overlap and at any time the area of staff activity and jurisdiction may need to be clarified and redefined. Usually trustee-staff relations are not difficult to define, particularly if they are kept on an informal, collegial level. There is, however, one major exception to the general ease of trustee-staff working relations, one area of potentially disruptive conflict in foundation practice. That issue is the procedure to be followed in the initiation of proposals and in negotiations with applicants.

It is both proper and advantageous in foundation program development for trustees to propose specific projects, provided that this is done directly to the board and in consultation with staff, and without prior entangling discussion with potential grant recipients. If competent staff has been employed, it is potentially disadvantageous for a trustee to negotiate or even discuss with a probable applicant the likelihood of favorable action should a particular grant request be submitted. Few persons can avoid, even with the firmest of intentions to be noncommittal, giving an impression of sympahy or disfavor in such a discussion. Any such impression is in effect a discourtesy to his trustee colleagues and a handicap to the staff in later processing the application if filed. It can also be a serious nuisance to the trustee himself if it becomes known that he is willing to engage in such backdoor, premature explorations. The effective response to such inquiries is a courteous referral to the staff with the explanation that this would be in accordance with trustee-determined procedure. An exception may be desirable if the contemplated proposal is definitely not within the foundation's area of activity and a prompt negative response would save time and trouble for all concerned. Unless the trustees of a foundation are sincerely convinced that its staff invariably should conduct the intermediary negotiations with all inquirers and applicants, naturally in consultation and with the aid of any trustee willing and able to help on occasion, only routine office workers should be employed. In fact, few if any superior foundation administrators will stay in a position if subjected to trustee circumvention. The trustee (perhaps an officer of the board) who prides himself on controlling "his" foundation by making decisions for which competent staff members have been employed will not only lose such staff members, but also will have undercut the morale of those persons while they are seeking other employment. Authority, once delegated, must be treated with respect.

Foundation legal counsel ordinarily is not regarded as part of the staff, but the function served is a staff function. Frequently the lawyer is the only professional serving a staff function. Even if there are lawyers on the board, it is good and common practice to employ outside counsel. Generally it is not advantageous for a foundation's counsel to serve as a board member, nor is it necessary to have him attend meetings of the board or its executive committee, although such relationships are not uncommon. Most matters discussed in meetings require no legal oversight. Only a few board actions need legal review before being given effect, and these may easily be checked in the minutes if counsel's advice has not been secured in advance by an alert foundation officer.

Lawyers are conspicuously overrepresented on boards of trustees. Yet the complexities of the laws relating to charitable trusts (briefly outlined in the preceding essay by Dr. Moore) are such that few lawyers have specialized competence in their interpretation and application. The historic, and still prevailing, doctrines of the common law, together with state and federal legislation, may rarely need to be called upon in current decisions. Yet occasionally such problems do arise. The attorneys on the board are unlikely to be experts on these abstruse matters, and the foundation's independent counsel may share their incompetence in these technicalities. More likely a foundation's lawyer will be an expert in the law and practice concerning estates or some aspect of business, industry, or finance. Socially permissible, prudent, and wise behavior in any one of these fields may be disadvantageously changed in character if followed by a foundation. For example, in 1952 a small number of the larger New York based foundations informally were asked by counsel for the Select Committee to Investigate Tax-Exempt Foundations and Comparable Organizations of the House of Representatives (Cox Committee) for full cooperation by voluntarily and freely reporting all their actions that might conceivably be questioned. The request was explained by the fact that the Select Committee had little money and time to complete its report. Lawyers for the foundations promptly advised against acceding to the request on the ground that it would be unwise from a foundation point of view and might invite a charge of collusion. To one untrained in the law this would seem sound advice if offered to a group of manufacturers or banks, for example, but unfortunate if followed by the trustees of tax-exempt funds dedicated to public benefit. It is a satisfaction to record that at least some of the lawyers later changed their minds and that in no case was the original advice followed by any of the foundations in question. Foundations as privileged trusts need legal advice that goes beyond their legal rights and obligations and takes account of their unique social responsibilities and opportunities.

The difficulty in the selection of foundation counsel and in knowing when to disregard advice if the wrong one has been chosen is further clarified in the following quotation from F. Emerson Andrews:

> . . . not the law, but particular lawyers have sometimes rendered a major disservice to philanthropy. Serving as trustees or legal advisors to foundations, they succeed in limiting programs of these organizations, not merely to what reasonable opinion would regard as within the law, but to innocuous acts which no one could question. To a distressing degree the grants of some foundations are determined, not upon the greatest public good, but upon sure avoidance of any possible tax question. The device

of tax exemption, which legislators designed to encourage and expand private enterprise in philanthropy, is sometimes being administered to constrict and imprison it.[21]

Burton Raffel, in criticizing the legal tendency to "track the statute," has observed that the purpose of The Rockefeller Foundation as stated in its charter, "to promote the well-being of mankind throughout the world," would not be likely to win the approval of most lawyers today, nor, it may be added, would it please the Internal Revenue Service.[22] On advice of counsel, many foundations restrict their grants to tax-exempt agencies listed in the federal *Cumulative List: Organizations Described in Section 170(c) of the Internal Revenue Code of 1954.* The Revenue Code does not demand such restrictions. Certainly grants may be made and are being made to individuals without an approved tax-exempt intermediary and to new agencies created for a special purpose of foundation interest, with due care that the purpose of the grant falls within the legally approved categories for foundation allocations. In sum, foundations with an innovative bent can be unnecessarily restricted because of overcautious legal advice more relevant to profit-making enterprise than to imaginative philanthropic endeavor. There is an unfortunate, if understandable, professional stance of lawyers with regard to any innovation: if in doubt, say, "No." And lawyers are often in doubt.

Whether or not a foundation is well staffed, much may be gained by tapping the wealth of experience and information relevant to its operations available from other foundations and advisory nonprofit organizations. However, many foundations, especially but not exclusively the smaller ones, fail to take advantage of this store of potentially helpful data and operate in isolation from the possible outside aid of colleagues and agencies created for their service. Such self-segregation has a variety of proffered defenses, none of unchallenged quality. Prominent among them are the traditional conviction that benev-

---

[21] F. Emerson Andrews, "Foreword," *UCLA Law Review*, vol. 13, May, 1966, p. 936.

[22] Burton Raffel, "Philanthropy and the Legal Mind: An Editorial," *Foundation News*, March, 1963, pp. 6–7.

olence should be a secret activity, the fear of stimulating a deluge of unwanted requests, and the possibility of a charge of belonging to an "interlocking network" of collusive portent. Although less often offered as a proper justification for seclusion, there is a natural desire to manage and allocate funds in trust in accordance with one's own predilections, frequently unchecked by any feeling of limited competence in benevolence. Yet in the past decade or so there has been a significant increase in inter-foundation discussion of mutual problems and experience, and with no observable reduction in the freedom of any foundation to exercise its own judgment.

It is, of course, true that foundations vary so greatly in objectives and procedures that any two may seem to have little more in common than a capital fund and a tax-free income. It is also, nevertheless, true that any one foundation can learn from others, or perhaps at least gain the satisfaction of assurance that comparatively it is doing a fine job in a fine way. That foundations increasingly are taking advantage of the possibility of learning from each other, although still only in comparatively small number, is evidenced by the growth of several agencies that facilitate inter-foundation communication.

The Foundation Center, previously mentioned as an example of inter-foundation cooperation in establishment and financing of an operating agency, was created in 1957 to serve both the general public and foundations as a source of all available information about foundations. It maintains a headquarters office and a library in New York City, a second office and library in Washington, D.C., and regional depositories in cooperation with universities and other institutions in Atlanta, Austin, Berkeley, Chicago, Cleveland, Kansas City, and Los Angeles. In addition to making available published materials on foundations and directly relevant to them and copies of foundation reports to the Treasury Department on Treasury Form 990-A, it also compiles and publishes a continuing list of foundations grants of $10,000 or more, publishes the bi-monthly *Foundation News*, prepares *The Foundation Directory* published by Russell Sage Foundation, undertakes studies in the foundation field, and offers consulting and professional training services for foundations. Most of the thousands of visits and written or telephoned inquiries annually received by the Center are from persons seeking information about foundations to which to submit proposals. This must be done from the records on file, for the Center will not suggest a particular foundation as likely or not to favor a particular project. Public officials, journalists, and scholars also are heavy users of the Center.

Most relevant for present purposes is the frequent use of the Center by foundation trustees and administrators for data and consultation on questions of foundation organization and management. Such use has been common on an informal basis from the start of the Center. A more formal consulting service for foundations with assigned staff and a panel of senior consultants was established in 1967 and is being widely used. The scope of consultation as stated in the Center's *Annual Report* for 1967 includes advice on ". . . problems of general organization, board responsibilities, administrative staffing, program planning and evaluation, and reporting."

Somewhat more specialized in background and interest are three national organizations that also are concerned with the effectiveness of foundation operation. The one with the broadest interest is the Council on Foundations, initially concerned mainly with foundations of the community trust type but since 1958 accepting affiliation by others, particularly family foundations. Membership now is open to any foundation tax exempt under Section 501(c)(3) or trust covered by Section 642(c) of the Internal Revenue Code of 1954. A staff director experienced in foundation activities heads the New York City office. Informative and well-attended annual conferences traditionally are held in various parts of the country. The nineteenth, in 1968, was held in Kansas City, Missouri. Published conference reports include the main addresses, always on subjects of basic interest to foundation trustees and administrators, and condensations of open discussions. Other materials relevant to foundation operation are prepared and distributed during the year. There is a membership fee that varies with foundation size and form of affiliation, but it is modest. About 350 foundations and community trusts are affiliated, not a large number when compared with the estimate of 22,000 foundations of all sizes existing in 1968, but a noteworthy indication of a growing desire on the part of a respectable number of foundation trustees and administrators to learn from their colleagues.

The Company Contribution Department of the National Industrial Conference Board concerns itself, as the name indicates, with corporate philanthropy, including company-sponsored foundations. It, too, has headquarters in New York City and holds conferences, makes studies, issues reports, and offers consultation. It long has been a positive influence in its field. Although its focus is on problems of a particular type of foundation, its activities are of broader interest. Corporate giving may differ in some respects from that of foundations which have received their corpus from individuals. The welfare of the parent company may not be left entirely out of account in its grants. A company-sponsored foundation is never freed of donor influence by death or otherwise. It dies if the company fails or if managerial policies no longer favor this form of philanthropy. As long as the foundation receives support, the source of that support will dominate. It is almost always a conduit foundation dependent on periodic contributions by the company and without expectation of large endowment. Yet foundations created by individuals also may be conduits dependent on gifts from time to time as the donor decides, subject to donor and the donor's heirs' influence, and possibly concerned with the welfare of the donor, as in the voting of stock in a company in which the donor is interested, or with his public image. The not uncommon attitude of trustees and administrators of privately funded foundations that their foundations are of a superior order and only distantly related to the company foundations can only be defended by comparison of the most distinguished of the one type with run-of-the-mill examples of the other. Acquaintance with the work of the National Industrial Conference Board's Company Contribution Department can be of particular benefit to those who administer family foundations, where the resemblance may be greatest.

The National Council on Philanthropy, originally the National Conference on Solicitations, was founded in 1954. As indicated by its prior title, the central interest is on relations between those in need of philanthropic funds and those who have them to disburse. The main participants are beneficiaries of benevolence and, on the foundation side, company-sponsored foundations.

There is less interest in foundation management as such than in the case of the two other national organizations just mentioned. Its stated purpose is the provision of a "national forum for donor and donee groups and others interested in the field of 'cooperative study of contribution problems, policies and procedures'." The proceedings of annual conferences are published and well worth review. The solicitor orientation should not cause one charged with foundation management to avoid what, after all, is the other side of his coin.

Less formal than the incorporated organizations suggested above as sources of information about foundation management are periodic and more casual conferences of donors, trustees, and administrators. The longest continuing and the prototype of such conferences on a regional basis is the Conference of Southwest Foundations held annually in the indicated part of the country, most often in Texas. There are formal addresses on foundation questions, some by persons distinguished in philanthropy from other parts of the country, and free discussions of practices and issues. Similar regional conferences have been held in California and the Midwest. The success of the educational role of the Conference of Southwest Foundations is so outstanding that it is hard to understand why similar continuing groups have not long since developed in all the main regions of the country. Although the addresses and discussions at the annual meetings of the Conference of Southwest Foundations have been remarkably informative and stimulating, the primary contribution in the opinion of many has been, as is so often the case with conferences, in the bringing together of donors, trustees, and administrators, many of them year after year, in congenial circumstances that encourage off-the-record conversation about experience, troublesome questions, achievements, and hopes. Getting acquainted, becoming accustomed to talking about philanthropy, an attendant weakening of the feeling that benevolence should be at least semi-private, and discovering that others may be helpful more than justifies the small expense and short time involved.

These incidental but most valuable by-products of well-organized conferences can be gained by even shorter and simpler meetings. For example, in New York City a very informal group of donors, trustees, and foundation administrators for years has held luncheon meetings once a month except in summer. There is a more or less formal after-lunch talk on some question of foundation operation or on some area of philanthropic interest, followed by questions and observations from the floor. Participants are associated with both the very large and the relatively small foundations. They come as individuals and not as foundation representatives. There is a hard core of regulars and a larger number of more casual participants. No records are kept. There are no dues and there are no rules except that no action may be taken other than the selection of a rotating steering committee. There is a cocktail period before lunch, and plenty of time then and during lunch for getting acquainted. Possibly the exceptional concentration of foundations in New York City explains why it is the only place where so large a group has so long continued. In other cities dependence for personal interchange probably has to be on more occasional meetings of smaller groups and on more personal contacts of individuals as a means for reducing the isolation of foundations and their personnel. Such casual contacts are common in New York City. The only firm ethical limitation on inter-foundation communication is that negative attitudes toward actual or potential applicants not be exchanged for fear of a kind of an unintentional "blacklisting" and of preventing a later fair hearing in terms of the objectives and standards of each foundation to which a request may be submitted.

Since 1953 New York University has held biennial conferences on charitable foundations as a forum ". . . at which foundation administrators and trustees and their tax advisors could meet to discuss problems of foundation organization, operation and philosophy."[23] Over the years, every conceivable subject of interest to foundation management has been reviewed by outstanding practitioners and scholars and debated by the rank and file of participants. Attendance, for which a reasonable fee is charged, is well worthwhile even for foundation personnel with long experience, both in terms of the information and the challenging views invariably presented and of the opportunities for contact with a wide range of colleagues. The full and well-edited reports

---

[23] Henry Sellin, editor, *Proceedings of the Seventh Biennial Conference on Charitable Foundations*, New York University (Albany, N.Y.: Matthew Bender & Co., Inc., 1965), p. iii.

are a mine of material on all aspects of foundation administration.

Foundation management, especially the management of the smaller and less well-staffed foundations, may need to turn to outside sources for information concerning applicant agencies. Is the organization under effective leadership? Is it well administered? Are its fund-raising and accounting practices all that they should be? Is it really needed? Can it make good use of more money and for the purpose stated? The last question may seem absurd. Who ever heard of an agency in a tax-exempt category that could not use more money? Yet there is one extreme case of a well-known agency of outstanding quality that for years has agreed that it has more money than it could use wisely in its charitable work, but it still receives a large total of unsolicited gifts each year. There are others that seek funds for questionable expansion. A distinguished scholar has observed that research, like a good hunting dog, should be kept a little on the lean side. Perhaps one might extend this to all philanthropic beneficiaries. With regard to the other questions, inadequate leadership and poor administration are not rare, nor are questionable fund-raising and accounting practices. Furthermore, some well-intentioned, high-minded agencies are to a serious degree redundant.

There is no better single source of basic information about national charitable agencies than the National Information Bureau in New York City, a nonprofit organization created to supply data to philanthropic donors, either individuals or foundations, who subscribe to its services. For information about local agencies, local services frequently are available, sometimes in association with community funds and councils, of which the Contributors' Information Bureau of the Community Council of Greater New York is an outstanding example. Such agencies can supply basic data that may be required to give assurance that a contemplated grant recipient is fundamentally sound. They can usually go much beyond that service in aid of trustee judgment on a proposal for support of something more specific and technical than general operations.

For more specialized data and advice the normal practice is to turn to referees and consultants, commonly on an ad hoc basis. However, qualified and reliable persons may be hard to find and difficult to select with confidence. It has been suggested that the task of proposal review might be given to an agency organized to serve a staff function for several foundations unable or unwilling to employ staff of their own. The suggestion that this be done on a commercial basis may be disregarded as both unsuitable and an unnecessary expense for philanthropic giving. However, there have been numerous instances when foundations have used agencies with investigative facilities on a commercial basis, including at least one known extreme case where a detective agency was employed by a trustee and its irrelevant report taken seriously by the board.

More persuasive is the argument that a multiple foundation advisory agency is needed to serve smaller foundations for a fee as needed. An agency available for processing proposals for any foundation for a reasonable charge and with no continuing tie to any foundation is not beyond reason or propriety. The main disadvantage of this type of service is the lack of continuous intimate foundation-agency relations to facilitate the agency's acquaintance with a foundation's objectives and requirements and to familiarize a foundation with the strengths, weaknesses, and possible biases of the agency. These disadvantages are less inherent in an agency operated for continuing service to a specific group of foundations, possibly selected with regard to some common interests such as a geographic area or broad category of potential beneficiaries. The *Annual Report* of the Foundation Library Center for 1967 includes a thoughtful essay entitled "Reflections on Foundations and the Future," unsigned, but evidently written by the president, Manning M. Pattillo, Jr., which predicts the development of this type of foundation cooperation:

> What about the thousands of small foundations that will be unable to employ professional directors? It is questionable whether a foundation with annual grants of less than $300,000 is justified in having a full-time administrator. The solution, I think, will be the formation of consortia—cooperative groups of small foundations, each to be administered by a salaried director. The Association of Foundations in Columbus, Indiana, and the Kansas City Association of Trusts and Foundations may be the prototypes. If the supply of experienced administrators can be increased and the approximately 18,000 small foundations organized into perhaps 1,000 associations with unified manage-

ment, remarkable strides can be made in the improvement of foundation programs in this country.

Dr. Pattillo seems too optimistic about the possibility of persuading foundations to enter into any kind of inter-foundation cooperation. Even though no delegation of any degree of authority concerning objectives and project decisions would be involved, merely turning over staff functions to a cooperative agency for many and probably most donors and trustees would be a painful diminution of the satisfaction derived from doing it all themselves. Few have any doubt about their present effectiveness. On the other hand, it may not be doubted that there are some who create or operate foundations who can be convinced of the desirability of joining forces with their counterparts as the advantages of administrative association are demonstrated.

One other source of extra-foundation educational and advisory help must not be overlooked, the foundation applicants. Here one must, of course, be wary, for all service-giving organizations and personnel are biased in favor of their particular fields of activity and of the importance and quality of their own work. They ought to be. Otherwise they should be in some other business. The common complaint by foundation trustees and administrators that every applicant is blindly convinced that his project should be given top priority by any reasonable person, reflects a failure to appreciate the fact that individual faith in the momentous promise of a proposal is a positive attribute of a candidate. Of course, sometimes applicants deliberately exaggerate the need for and the effectiveness of their services to the point of being misleading if not guilty of actual prevarication. Still, properly winnowed, the information to be obtained from applicants by observation of their operations and by frank and probing discussion is hard to equal by less direct inquiry.

In the preceding pages stress has been put on the roles of staff and extra-foundation sources of data and advice because neglect and conscious avoidance of both, rather than the oft-repeated charges of self-dealing and undermining of the American way of life, have been the major but publicly overlooked weaknesses of foundations. Indeed, there has been strong criticism of foundations for making use of such help, as though it were akin to abdication of responsibility. How else can trustees, largely laymen in the fields of their foundations' activities, meet their responsibility to expend the funds at their disposal effectively for the benefit of the public? A comment attributed to the late William McPeak, a former vice-president of The Ford Foundation, bitingly expresses concern about the necessity for foundation decisions to be based on adequate information. In paraphrase, he agreed that foundations should be venturesome, but only with sufficient informed care that although there might be understandable failure, at least it should be as certain as humanly possible that a grant would do no harm.

If it seems unlikely that a solicited cash grant could do harm, there may be cited as one type of example to the contrary the numerous instances of grievous distress in basic operations and budget suffered by overambitious charities and academic institutions because of commonly overlooked extra costs, unexpected interference with ongoing programs, and unconsidered responsibilities following termination of support, all of which may be by-products of special projects financed by foundations with the best of intentions and complete self-satisfaction. Grants also may be unfortunate from broader economic and social welfare points of view, but that is a question reserved for later consideration.

Financial Policies and Administration

Technically, the financial responsibilities of trustees of tax-exempt foundations may be summed up as the assurance of the availability of the maximum amount of money for furthering approved objectives within the limits of the donor's mandate and the laws and regulations of the federal and relevant state governments. Unlike the directors of business corporations, they have no obligation to make money other than by ordinary investment dividends and interest. No less important than their strictly defined financial responsibilities as set by law are the extra-legal dictates of ethical standards and the expectation of the public that as managers of public trusts they will not engage in or even permit any semblance of devious sharp practice.

Tax Exemption. The remission of taxes on legally specified benevolent donations is taken for granted in the United States not only as proper, but also virtually as a social necessity and natural right. This view is so thoroughly embedded in the culture of this country that it is a sharp surprise for most Americans when they learn that it is not universal or at least the common view also of our European contemporaries. Yet ". . . the tax and other inducements which so greatly encourage giving in the United States are extremely limited, or do not exist, in most of Europe. Gifts from individuals are not tax-deductible at all in Austria, Belgium, Norway, Sweden, Switzerland; nor in England except under a complicated seven-year covenant agreement."[24] American federal, state, and local tax exemptions for benevolence in their liberal allowances and in the wide variety of permissible objectives are unique government subsidies of private philanthropy. Nevertheless, foundation trustees need vigorously to reject and combat the very common belief that the funds in their charge are "taxpayers' dollars." Foundation assets are not largely taken from the taxpayers' pockets. *The Foundation Directory, Edition 3* lists 297 foundations still in existence that were founded before 1930, of which 26, including The Rockefeller Foundation, Carnegie Corporation of New York, The Duke Endowment, and Russell Sage Foundation, had assets in the early years of $10,000,000 or more. Estate, gift, and income taxes either did not exist or were very low at the time of establishment of these foundations. Their endowment cost the taxpayer nothing or very little. Since they still exist, it may be said that they at least are using money presently that in other hands would be subject to income tax, but what their income taxes would be if taxed at the prevailing corporation rate is another matter.

If foundation assets were taxed at the prevailing rates for gifts and bequests by individuals at the time of donation and at corporation rates for annual income, the question is how much would the government receive in additional taxes? This is a difficult question to answer. It is impossible to answer with exactitude because there is no way of knowing what alternative uses might be made of the funds if so taxed.

With regard to gift and estate taxes on endowments, unless

---

[24] F. Emerson Andrews, "The Fifth Freedom," *The Bulletin of the American Association of Fund-Raising Counsel, Inc.*, vol. 12, February, 1966, p. 1.

tax exemption were also denied all charitable, educational, and religious bodies, it is probable that there would be a considerable number of alternative gifts and bequests to welfare agencies, colleges, universities, churches, and church-supported institutions. These operating agencies after all are representative of the places foundation funds are intended for eventually, only on a slower schedule, with greater flexibility and with the broader concern of an intermediary board of trustees. The major doubt about this likelihood relates to endowments strongly motivated by a desire to keep control of a business in family hands by giving stock in it to a family-controlled foundation. This doubt loses force when it is realized that it is not impossible or even difficult to find a tax-exempt operating agency able and willing to serve the same purpose by holding shares in a successful business indefinitely and voting them for management.

The amount of tax money that would be collected by applying the prevailing income-tax provisions for corporations also would be much smaller than is generally believed. Corporation income derived from dividends on stock in other corporations is 85 per cent exempt from income tax. The proportion of total foundation assets invested in corporate shares is high, these days rarely dropping below something in the order of 60 per cent and not infrequently exceeding 90 per cent.[25] Ordinary operating expenses, of course, are deductible from the income-tax base, as also are charitable gifts up to 5 per cent of income. Foundations that operate programs directly with their own staff could deduct the costs. Foundations with operating programs currently are very few, but their number might be expected to increase in the event of an income-tax levy. Also to be kept in mind when considering the loss of government income because of foundation tax exemption is the dollar saving by the government because of foundation support of health, welfare, and educational activities that otherwise would be a government responsibility.

A question that seems never to have been raised formally and has not been answered as a matter of law asks what is the net

---

[25] For an analysis of the investments and financial management of the fifty largest foundations and samplings of company-sponsored and community foundations, see Ralph L. Nelson, previously cited.

income of a foundation that has spent all of its gross income for the philanthropic purposes for which it was chartered. Dean Rusk, while president of The Rockefeller Foundation, commented on this question most intriguingly. After pointing out that such tax-exempt institutions as colleges and universities ordinarily had no net income after "doing the only business for which they are chartered" and recognizing that distinguished legal authorities would disagree, he went on to say that "Even in the case of such a foundation as ours, when we get through doing in the course of a year the only business for our being, which is philanthropy, we have no income tax. We have no income. We think that there might be very serious problems under the sixteenth amendment, the income-tax amendment, if a Congress should attempt to impose an income tax on what might be called our gross income."[26] At present there is no impelling need to test the legality of this view. Tax exemption may continue to be regarded as a government subsidy, but not nearly so great a one as commonly alleged.

The practical significance of foundation tax exemption is not that income available for beneficiaries would seriously be reduced should it be terminated. It lies rather in its anti-foundation propaganda misuse in the charge that foundation money is largely a taxpayer subsidy and in its availability as a legal basis for federal supervision to assure compliance with relevant legislation. Tax exemption is an affirmation of the American fundamental belief in and respect for private giving in aid of others. Reflecting this public attitude, the legislative trend increasingly has favored all forms of private benevolence, including foundations. This fact commonly is overlooked largely because of the publicity given criticisms of foundations by a few congressmen offering a minimum of supporting data and concerning a very few foundations whose misbehavior deserved castigation. Tax exemption is a convenience in the flexibility and the relatively few extra dollars it affords. It also is a minor nuisance as a foothold for overly extended Internal Revenue Service surveillance and for poorly informed critics in Congress and elsewhere. Yet it is of benefit to

[26] Dean Rusk, *The Role of the Foundation in American Life* (Claremont, Calif.: Claremont University College, 1961), pp. 17–18.

well-managed foundations and the public as a legal source of authority for the correction of the abuse of the foundation form of philanthropy for personal gain. Tax exemption is a mixed privilege, but unquestionably advantageous for all concerned: donors, foundations, beneficiaries, government, and society.

Prudence in Investment.   Security of the capital fund from loss by unfortunate investment is always a major responsibility of foundation trustees. Imprudent financial speculation is a charge no trustee wishes to face. Nor does any trustee wish to face the possibility of a surcharge action being brought against him because of excessively risky financial transactions. Caution for the protection of corpus is both obligatory and commendable, but may be questioned if its purpose merely is the preservation of the number of dollars in the original endowment. Such a purpose does not take into account the likelihood of disastrous consequences of inflation on the fulfillment of a foundation's mandate, nor does it allow for increasing need for foundation activity in a growing and changing society. Neither the law nor the public will take critical action if investment is only in gilt-edged bonds with no possibility of capital growth, even though there always is a possibility of decline in dollar as well as relative value in any such security. Management of endowments with timidity that disregards economic and social trends, though safe from a trustee's personal point of view, is not unqualifiedly commendable.

Combined concern both for security of corpus and capital growth is the genuinely prudent financial policy for a foundation because of its conformity with economic and social reality. It reduces the danger of creeping ineffectiveness through decline in dollar value and the swelling of philanthropic needs. On the other hand, it has a disadvantage in the minds of many in that growth investments usually yield lower immediate returns and thus to some extent reduce possible current aid to present beneficiaries. The dilemma in which trustees may find themselves in deciding on the relative emphasis to give current and future income may only be solved by reference to their chartered purpose and their own estimate of current and longer term social requirements.

Investment in exceptionally low-income yielding stock or nonproductive tangible property in comparison with holdings that produce reasonable returns and also have good growth prospects is a questionable indirect form of income accumulation. Although currently legal, it is not easy to defend in view of the legal rule against income accumulation. The Internal Revenue Code provides that tax exemption shall be denied a foundation for that year in which its accumulated income "is unreasonable in amount or duration." (The implementing regulations exclude capital gains in determining the unreasonableness of accumulations, but are somewhat indefinite about what may be considered unreasonable. Courts have shown a tendency to favor foundations when a dispute with the Internal Revenue Service about the limits of unreasonableness is brought before them.) It is an omen worth most serious trustee consideration that the Treasury Department has taken the position that:

> The ability to increase the size of a nonoperating foundation's corpus by withholding a current benefit from the public is as much an abuse when it takes the form of an indirect accumulation as when it takes the form of a direct accumulation. . . . To insure that all private nonoperating foundations provide at least a minimum current benefit to charity it is recommended that there be established a "floor" below which the current benefits provided by the foundation to the public would not be permitted to drop. Such an approach could provide that if a private nonoperating foundation's income, and therefore its required payment to charity under the direct-accumulation proposal, falls below a specified percentage of the value of its holdings, the foundation would have to pay to charity, from its corpus, an amount which would approximate the income which it would have received had it invested its funds in the type of assets held by comparable organizations.[27]

Present Versus Future Interests. The theoretical justification for this Treasury Department recommendation is that tax exemption and public benefit should be as nearly concurrent as reasonably

---

[27] *Treasury Department Report on Private Foundations* (Washington: Government Printing Office, 1965), p. 28. Without implying agreement with everything in this report, it is recommended for reading by foundation trustees and administrators as a thoughtful review of the problems of foundation financial management of critical concern to legislators, Treasury Department officials, and many private citizens.

possible, a difficult argument to counter. The same theoretical position may be taken with regard to the exemption from taxation to the individual or his estate of contributions to a foundation where, as the Treasury Department points out, ". . . there is usually a significant lag between the time of the contribution, with its immediate effect upon tax revenues, and the time when the public benefits by having an equivalent amount of funds devoted to charitable activities."[28] Yet there is much to be said for taking a longer view, for recognizing that the present has some responsibility for the future. One may grant that indirect accumulation of income is as much an abuse as direct accumulation, as the Treasury Department argues, but that only raises the question why direct accumulation in itself requires absolute prohibition by all grant-making foundations. The Treasury Department should not be interpreted as recommending risky maximization of income, for it suggests only 3 to 3 and one-half per cent of the market value of assets as the "floor" for foundation annual expenditures. What is difficult to accept is the Department's assumption and that of the Congress as expressed in legislation that current activity of all foundations is more important for the public than longer-run planning and effort. The argument that "accumulating income does nothing to relieve the burdens of government"[29] advanced in an action against The Danforth Foundation ignores the best interests of beneficiaries and the fact that public sentiment favors tax exemption for philanthropic agencies primarily because of concern for human welfare rather than possible reduction of government expenditures.

The same assumption of the primacy of the present underlies the argument that foundation trustees should not hesitate to invade capital or even spend all capital and go out of business in a comparatively few years if permitted by the terms of establishment. This is good advice for smaller foundations unable to attract trustees of the needed quality and philanthropic interests after the death of the donor or unable to afford the employment of suitable staff. Under such circumstances there is a tendency to

---

[28] *Ibid.*, p. 24.

[29] Danforth Foundation vs. U.S., 222 F. Supp. 761 (D.C.Mo. 1963). Quoted in Marion R. Fremont-Smith, previously cited, p. 177.

make routine grants of random personal interest to trustees and an inability to adjust programs to changing social needs and opportunities. Yet such circumstances have no real relevance to the questionable assumption that only current interests are important.

If a foundation is large enough to be free of the management limitations inherent in small size, the two common arguments raised against long life for foundations do not seem compelling. The view that foundation concentrations of great wealth place too much power in the hands of too few people and are dangerous for the economic and social order may be debated both as a matter of fact and as a conflict of individual values. To whatever extent it may have validity, remedies are readily at hand through federal and state legislation, as in the case of similar possible dangers inherent in the far greater concentrations of wealth managed by the directors of giant corporations.

The other argument that foundations with unlimited life allow the dead hand of the past to reach dangerously into the future or just lie around uselessly takes for granted that mandates are narrow and inflexible, as they are not for most foundations today, particularly the larger ones, or that trustees are limited in vision, which has too often been the case, but far from always. If trustees' vision is myopic, the remedy needs to be specific and not applied to all foundations indiscriminately. The fact is that the programs of the larger foundations can be and frequently are altered to keep up with the times. Program change is practically inevitable as permitted by charter or deed of trust, both because of the quality of the majority of their trustees and administrators and because of the compelling force of social change and example. It would be a serious social loss if large foundations voluntarily or by government decree terminated their activities in consequence of largely spectral dangers capable of remedy by less drastic remedies insofar as they may have substance in specific cases.

Relatively minor invasions of corpus that do not cripple a foundation's ongoing operations from time to time may be desirable. They may or may not be recouped from later income, depending on trustee judgment of long-term need for corpus restoration. Quite ordinarily in recent years they have been automatically more than replaced by capital gains with no need to curtail expenditures from dividends and interest. Foundations of huge size need not be concerned about expending some capital when exceptional opportunity too costly to accept otherwise is presented. The main corpus-invasion problem for trustees of great foundations is that always there are so many costly opportunities, as for buildings and endowment, gleaming in the eyes of persuasive managers of hospitals, universities, museums, and other philanthropic institutions, that there are continual temptations to cut into corpus past the point where it hurts. Some of the foundations of intermediate size have found protection against grandiose grantsmanship in adopting a standing rule against capital expenditures. Such a rule would seem inappropriate for the very largest foundations where the preservation of every dollar of endowment obviously is unnecessary from any point of view.

Restriction of appropriations to income may be regretted because of enticing opportunities lost for want of adequate available funds. This is inevitable except for the very largest foundations. There are, however, two intermediate alternatives to the extreme positions (the extreme positions being invasion of capital or confinement of expenditures strictly to income from interest, dividents, or other current investment returns). One alternative is to spend capital gains, if any, rather than accumulate them, if there is no strong reason for guarding against inflation. A foundation of very small size or with very delimited, and finite, objectives may have no reason for taking a very long view of its capital resources. There also is much to recommend a policy of defining as "funds available for appropriation" at any particular board meeting some proportion of the total income anticipated over several years in advance. Carnegie Corporation of New York permits commitment of anticipated income five years in advance up to 50 per cent of the expected revenues. Such a rule assumes that payments of grants to some extent will be spread over about the same number of years. There is, of course, some risk that income may be reduced precipitously. Even so, adjustment can be made by reducing new allocations. (It is, of course, a little awkward for a foundation's officers and trustees to have little or no money to spend for a period, but that situation does provide an excellent basis for declining to support a project of dubious merit.) The alternative of restricting commitments to income in hand or practically certain within the fiscal year has no element of risk and is the more general practice, perhaps for that reason.

A grant to be paid over a period of several years may be charged against anticipated income over the same period. Yet such a policy, particularly if it commits a large proportion of expected income, runs the obvious risk that the income may not be forthcoming, and the subtle risk that the trustees and staff may have little excuse for their positions over the period when no new decisions are to be made. Thus keeping commitments on a current basis, with grants charged to current income regardless of payment periods, is a defensible practice. Nevertheless, it is arguable that paying grant installments out of the income in the year it is received rather than out of prior income held from the time of the commitment is also "keeping current."

Decision on basic financial policy concerning relative emphasis on income and corpus, an emphasis that is likely to need modification from time to time, clearly requires a continuous series of subsidiary decisions in investment practice. These are subject to federal and state laws and regulations governing foundation financial transactions and also need to be guided by less formal but no less compelling principles of business ethics and a discriminating perception of fiduciary propriety.

Unrelated Business and Improper Transactions. The broad underlying legal requirement that "reasonable diligence, care and prudence" must be exercised by trustees in a fiduciary position, the "prudent man" doctrine, is of little more than admonitory help in practical decisions. It permits and may stimulate overcautious investment erosive of capital and lacks specificity in its threat of potential suit for mismanagement. Foundations are not restricted to "legal list" securities except in the case of charitable trusts in a few states. Thus the range of "prudent" choice is wide. State legislation varies too greatly for any attempt at generalization beyond the comment that the "prudent man" doctrine applies everywhere. Federal investment restrictions applying to all foundations and charitable trusts deny tax exemption to the conduct of an unrelated trade or business and forbid transactions that are self-serving to some categories of persons associated with foundations.

The Internal Revenue Codes of 1950 and 1954 impose a tax on foundations and charitable trusts that engage in a trade or business not substantially related to the ongoing activities for which tax exemption was granted. So-called "feeder corporations," that is, business organizations all of whose income is committed to a charitable agency, also have been denied tax exemption since 1950. Income received as interest, dividends, annuities, royalties, and, to some extent, rents specifically are not included as coming from an unrelated trade or business. Prior to 1950 it was not unusual for tax-exempt agencies to own a variety of money-making businesses such as stores or manufacturing plants with the advantage of tax-free income from them. The loss of taxes from such businesses, and the very serious competitive disadvantage suffered by profit-oriented enterprises have been viewed by the Congress, quite reasonably, as outweighing the advantage of the extra funds that otherwise would be available for public charitable purposes.

There remains, however, a considerable area of doubt about the precise meaning of the phrase "not substantially related." The profitable operation of a farm or dairy by an agricultural college definitely is substantially related to the tax-exempt purpose of the college, but just how big need be the farm, the herd of cows, or the milk-processing plant adequately to serve the college's purpose? The insistence of the Internal Revenue Service that gain from advertising in a journal published by a professional society such as the American Medical Association or the American Association for the Advancement of Science is taxable as not substantially related to tax-exempt purpose seems debatable. Just how much business activity is permissible as not substantial and just what business is truly unrelated in a specific case remain only vaguely defined other than at the extremes by law, judicial decision, or the rulings of the Internal Revenue Service. A result of this lack of clear definition is that there are many tempting opportunities for foundation investment of uncertain propriety.

All transactions prohibited by federal law to prevent the misuse of foundations for private gain are also violations of good moral judgment or good taste. A foundation in its relations with a donor or a substantial contributor, a member of the family of either, or a corporation controlled by either, may not lend money except with proper security and at a reasonable rate of interest, pay compensation other than for actual service and at a reasonable rate, give preferential service, buy or sell securities or other property in substantial amount except for adequate consideration, or do anything else resulting in a diversion of its funds. It would be hard to challenge these restrictions, except on the ground that some of the terms are vague and that the categories to which they apply are insufficiently extensive. How are "reasonable," "adequate," "preferential," and "substantial" to be defined? Donors, contributors, their families, and controlled businesses do not include all who might well be proscribed as parties to such transactions. Why not employers and employees, partners, and even cronies? Granted that it may be impractical to devise an all-inclusive list, at least the present one could be somewhat extended. In any event, all of the listed prohibited transactions are contrary to sound business practice and should be regarded as violations of trust no matter with whom they may be made. As presently stated in the law, they are a redundant minimum and may give an appearance of lower standards than prevail in other trust relationships. When complete freedom of arm's-length and inconsequential business dealings with foundations is added to the inadequacies of the law concerning unrelated business, the result is a large area of uncertainty for trustee financial decision.

There are many blending shades of gray between black and white. So it is with the great variety of legally permissible foundation financial transactions. Without any attempt to list all possible dubious kinds of transactions or describe any one in detail, a few of those most commonly questioned may be selected for illustration. Is it proper for a foundation to make direct commercial loans either at the prevailing rate of interest or perhaps slightly lower because of the advantage of not using an intermediary? If so, should they be restricted to borrowers in the United States or extend to overseas governments, banks, and business enterprises? If this is improper, is it also improper to offer mortgage money without the aid of an intermediary agency? Should a foundation take advantage of the possibility of increasing capital gains by security purchases and sales for that primary purpose, the so-called "churning" of investments? Should long-term investment for capital growth with lower current income than otherwise might be obtainable be penalized by requiring compensating payments out of capital, as previously discussed? Owning and operating an unrelated business is legal and the income is taxable, but should it be avoided because of possible abuses? Is borrowing for investment rather than for immediate program needs always unwise?

Is there some limit to the proportion of corpus properly held in one investment? Numerous foundations have been endowed with a large block of shares in a single corporation. Should such blocks be held indefinitely if financially sound and profitable, thus undertaking the risk of having all eggs in one basket and giving the donor, if (as usual) he is a member or represented on the board of trustees, possible control of the company? Should a foundation actively take sides in a proxy fight by voting its shares as a donor, trustee, or finance committee desires? Should an unproductive gift, such as a valuable painting, estate, white-elephant town house or vacant land, be accepted without a definite agreement that it will be sold promptly if not usable in the foundation's program? This is not an exhaustive list of gray area questions, nor does it include the ingenious variations in practice devised with expert legal advice more for the benefit of donors than for foundation advantage. It may be that the public fiduciary nature of foundations requires that they be above all suspicion and justifies the criticisms made when any gray area transaction becomes known.

The common interpretation of such transactions as motivated by purely selfish expectation of personal gain by the donor or trustees requires verification case by case. Radically differing honest opinions about what is or is not in the public interest are held by sincere philanthropists. Differing opinions concerning the variety of legally permissible financial transactions by foundations flow from differing prime concerns of the parties at interest. The Treasury Department and its Internal Revenue Service, as one party, have the duty of enforcing the relevant acts of Congress and of preventing tax evasion by collecting every dollar due. It also has the duty on occasion of advising the Congress as well as the federal administration on how things are going and on what legislative improvements, in its opinion, might be made. The public, represented by the Congress and the administration, has a broad interest in all classes of potential beneficiaries of philanthropy that is not always compatible with its interests of an economic and political nature. Foundation financial interest must by virtue of the fiduciary role be concerned about maximizing resources, while being mindful of the larger interests of society. Potential beneficiaries, whether operating agencies or the ultimate recipients of aid, also have an interest in maximizing philanthropic funds both in amount and in effectiveness in distribution. Reconciliation of such divergent priorities of interest may only be in the form of compromise, not a compromise adopted once and for all but one in continuing adaptive flux.

Federal administrative concern with foundation finances as reflected by the *Treasury Department Report on Private Foundations* to the Committee on Finance of the United States Senate[30] seems to be almost exclusively with foundations' relations to the national economy and tax collection, as affected by the abuses of the foundation mechanism for private gain by both tax avoidance and tax evasion. The main mention of beneficiaries in the report is in a seven-page section entitled "Delay of Benefit to Charity," and even in this section there is more evident concern about tax collection than for the needs of beneficiaries. This is understandable in view of the Treasury Department's proper function; nevertheless, it leaves charity without an administrative spokesman. The same also is true of the reports of the chairman (Representative Wright Patman) to the Select Committee on Small Business (87th Congress) and to its Subcommittee No. 1 on Foundations entitled *Tax-Exempt Foundations and Charitable Trusts* and of the later hearings before the Subcommittee. Of course, a Select Committee on Small Business may be expected to focus on its stated subject, but the contents of the voluminous reports already issued suggest a much broader concern than small business without serious attention to beneficiary needs.[31]

---

[30] Washington: Government Printing Office, 1965.

[31] "The bulk of these [Patman] reports is tremendous. Although additions are probably still to come, the published documentation (excluding numer-

The two earlier Congressional inquiries about foundations, chaired by Representative Eugene E. Cox (82nd Congress, 1952) and Representative B. Carroll Reece (83rd Congress, 1954) were more concerned with the impact of foundations on "the American way of life," as was the Commission on Industrial Relations established by the 62nd Congress in 1912 and chaired by Frank P. Walsh. It may be that foundations and their beneficiaries are too diverse in areas of activity and too few as voters to stir up active governmental support.

Foundations may appear in regular courts as plaintiffs (usually in *cy pres* actions to change the terms of a bequest) or as defendants (for various alleged abuses). In the quasi-judicial proceedings of Congressional committees, the foundations have also had their day in court, but always as defendants. The instigators of such investigatory hearings are not motivated by an attempt to display the good that foundations may do, or even to elicit information and policies in a neutral atmosphere. Though specifically charitable in chartered purpose, and thus benefactors, foundations are treated by investigative committees of Congress as a special category of "malefactors of great wealth."

The problem of reconciliation of diverse interest priorities is evident in all gray area disputes, and shows up with particular clarity in arguments about the propriety of foundation transactions for income and capital growth from "active" rather than from "passive" investments. It has been noted that income from an "unrelated trade or business" is taxed. Ownership of a business with or without the assumption of active management duties, fully taxed, is frowned upon. One may even expect to hear cavils and queries about the operation of a clearly related activity, such as the publication of the findings of foundation-financed studies. In the nature of the prospective market, most such publications

---

ous items in *Congressional Record*) already run to some 4,200 pages in six *Report* 'installments' and two volumes of *Hearings*."

See F. Emerson Andrews, *Patman and Foundations: Review and Assessment* (New York: The Foundation Center, 1968), p. 5. This 62-page pamphlet contains brief accounts of earlier Congressional investigations of foundations as well as a succinct evaluation of Congressman Patman's inquiry. It includes a bibliography listing the basic documents and relevant general publications.

are of scant interest to commercial publishers, for the books are, in effect, subsidized by the publishing foundation. Yet an occasional title, also the outcome of a foundation-supported undertaking, would prove attractive to a commercial publisher. Invariably, such works are selected by ordinary publishers as examples of improper competition. An occasional author, commissioned and paid to do a technical study, regrets that he cannot also collect royalties on his printed product. Clearly in these circumstances the trustees and staff of a foundation must adopt a fairly "hard line"; they will not engage in an "unrelated business" (such as publishing unsolicited manuscripts based on unsupported research), and the few that wish to do so retain the right to publish the outcome of supported research. The noise about unfair competition in these circumstances is, on inspection, noisome.

There are many responsible people in government, in foundation management, and in the public generally who believe strongly that foundations should not involve themselves "actively" in any economic operation for financial gain. They hold that capital should be invested solely in securities and property managed by others independent of the foundation. Dividends, interest, and rents from foundation-owned property managed by others, together with capital gains more or less incidental in nature, constitute the sources of foundation income that arouse no fault-finding in consequence of source. Those who object to "active" foundation income define the word broadly to include direct loans with proper security and reasonable interest, sound mortgages not purchased through an intermediary, rents from property not managed by an independent real estate firm or specialist, borrowing to take advantage of an attractive investment opportunity, frequent turnover of securities for capital gains, and taking sides in a stockholder contest for control of a corporation in which there is an investment. Few will argue that a foundation should be permitted to enter the marketplace with its tax exemption as a competitive weapon. Insofar as this still may be done by ingenious sharp practice, as in the "boot strap" purchase of a closely held business by payment out of later income from the business and under conditions of agreement affording tax advantage to both the seller and the foundation, no adequate defense can be offered. Such devious tax avoidance is contrary to the intent of existing legislation and questionable on ethical grounds.[32]

Aside from legal chicanery, which will almost certainly receive due attention from the Internal Revenue Service, if not from the attorneys general and other state authorities where the power properly belongs, many issues remain unresolved. As the law now appears to stand, involvement in improper and unfair production of "active" income for foundations is still subject to some pointed criticism. It is argued, for example: that the production of "active" income both permits and induces sharp practice and downright abuse of foundation privileges; that such ventures involve foundations in needlessly risky speculation with their funds; that playing the speculative market may in fact result in a conflict of interest between the chartered purpose of a foundation and the private purposes of donors or trustees; that deep and active involvement in rather speculative investments may well distract foundation trustees and salaried staff from their primary, philanthropic mission; and, finally, that such risk-taking may be unfair to private enterprise. (We cannot enter here on a discussion of the effect of "institutional investors" on stock markets. We can only note that, with respect to most foundations—as compared with mutual funds, insurance companies, and private pension trusts—charitable organizations are likely to have at most minor or unwitting effects, and by virtue of their mode of management are in no way able to manipulate market prices of holdings.)

Abuses defined as contrary to law, the public will, and strict ethical standards should be prohibited, of course. Distraction from philanthropic duties is not an inevitable occurrence, but may happen and should be censured when it does. Speculation and conflicts of interest can and will be avoided by responsible trustees and should be penalized when allowed to occur. The nub of the matter is less altruistic. It is that self-appointed representatives of private enterprises are concerned that such business

---

[32] For examples of the devious ways in which foundation tax exemption may be of competitive financial advantage to the owner of a business and to a foundation, see the previously cited *Treasury Department Report on Private Foundations*.

concerns should get the fees and profits obtainable from "active income" transactions. It is difficult to think of any reason that banks, mortgage brokers, or managers of real estate should have exclusive rights in foundation transactions in their several fields which would not extend similarly to the production of income by churches, academic institutions, labor unions, welfare agencies, and other tax-exempt organizations.

As of now, a foundation legally may invest its funds in about any way a man of wealth may use his capital, as long as it avoids violating the prudent man rule governing investment for others and not for self and does not engage in any of the "prohibited transactions" previously mentioned. The laws on unrelated business and on prohibited transactions do need clarification and tightening to eliminate tricky and sometimes unethical avoidance practices by a minority of donors and foundation trustees, contrary to Congressional intent, and contrary to the long evolution of the rules of trusteeship. Those who argue that the production of "active" income is an evasion of the unrelated business prohibition ignore the distinction between the use of tax exemption as an advantage in market-place competition for other people's business and the saving of money by the direct and prudent conduct of a foundation's own ordinary operation. There would be a significant difference between income derived, let us say, from ownership of a department store in competition for the customers of Macy's and Gimbel's if it were tax-free and that derived from a direct loan to the same hypothetical store, properly secured and at reasonable interest. There would be no criticism if the same amount of money were made available to the same store in the form of a bond purchase on the open market, a condition that suggests a cynical interpretation.

Not all of the nuances of such situations are legally or ethically clear. The main point is that a charitable foundation's investments should not *significantly* alter private managerial policies or private competitive positions in financial or consumer markets. It would be ridiculous to suppose that the investment transactions of foundations have no effect on the markets for money and equities. They must, as do all other investment transactions. What foundations are forbidden to do is a kind of action freely available to the individual investor if he has the requisite financial resources, and that is to change the shape of the market, of the competitive pattern among claimants to the investor's dollar-charged confidence. Because foundations have unique privileges and public functions, they must, of course, be held to special standards. Even so, there is no clear reason for prohibiting direct investments (under limiting assumptions already noted); dealing through an intermediary will not necessarily clean up the transaction, and may simply make it less rewarding.

There is one way of seeking "active" investment income which requires separate consideration, that sought from investments with both a financial and a philanthropic purpose. Student loans on terms easier than obtainable on the open market are one example. Loans and other forms of aid in the establishment of small businesses by members of disadvantaged groups have been found attractive by a number of philanthropists. Housing for the disadvantaged seems to have been the most attractive of such dual objective ventures. Apartment houses have been built for low-income families and those suffering from ethnic discrimination; run-down houses have been renovated and low rental new houses have been built by dual purpose corporations. Many such ventures have been either financial misfortunes or without noteworthy philanthropic accomplishment. Some have fallen short of both objectives.

Low-yield investment in a project that private enterprise would avoid at a higher rate of return should be classified as high-risk speculation. Probably most such projects have been so regarded despite confident announcements that capital would be recovered and some small interest earned. Such investment should be regarded as a contingent grant. Mrs. Russell Sage showed sensitivity to the difficulty of effectively combining investment and social betterment objectives by restricting investment "for the improvement of social and living conditions" to not more than one-quarter of her initial gift to Russell Sage Foundation and requiring that such investment "shall, in the opinion of the trustees, be likely to produce an annual income of not less than three per cent."[33] The Ford Foundation has taken the realistic position that "Purchase of securities for other than investment reasons to

---

[33] Letter of Gift, April 19, 1907.

implement social objectives should be considered grants and administered by the grant authorities."[34] Not only the purchase of securities, but also the purchase of any other property should be so regarded.

More discouraging than the financial risk is the not uncommon minor philanthropic accomplishment. Forest Hills Gardens on Long Island, a Russell Sage Foundation project intended to offer improved housing for relatively low-income white collar workers in New York City, both lost money and turned out to be too expensive for the intended beneficiaries. It was a project that well illustrates the problems typical of dual purpose ventures, for, with hindsight, it is easy to see that there was an inherent conflict between the plan to regain capital with a low interest return and the intention to provide garden community housing not commercially feasible under the circumstances. Still, dual purpose projects can be dually successful. The Provident Loan Society was established to aid the financially distressed in avoiding loan sharks by providing a place where the poor could obtain needed cash quickly by pawning some possession of value on reasonable terms and with confidence that the terms would be met. It was financed by the philanthropically motivated purchase of certificates of contribution permitting returns limited to 6 per cent "when and if earned and declared." These have been fully paid. The *New York Times* reported in its September 29, 1968, issue that The Ford Foundation has announced that it will ". . . place part of its investment portfolio in ventures aiding the poor and minority groups and land conservation rather than in enterprises offering greater financial return" and that ". . . at least 10 prominent foundations are considering a joint undertaking similar to the unilateral effort by Ford." Extra care is required in the consideration of such ventures that there is no glossing over of financial risks because of enthusiasm for the desired humanitarian gain. If there is financial doubt and the philanthropic objective is appealing, the only justifiable responses to such proposals are either acceptance of the risk inherent in aspiration for the accomplishment of two unrelated objectives by one transaction or a regretful declination.

---

[34] Ralph L. Nelson, previously cited, p. 99.

The size and circumstances of acquisition of a foundation's security holdings in a single corporation are of serious concern to the public as well as to the foundation's trustees. Broad diversification of investments generally is accepted as the proper foundation policy both because of the reduction in risk of crippling loss and because of the advisability of avoiding criticism based on fear of abuse of corporation control by a philanthropic enterprise. One exemplary but possibly overcautious large foundation limits its ownership in any corporation to not more than one per cent of the corporation's securities and not more than five per cent of its own principal fund. Where the upper limit may best be set is a matter of judgment relative to the circumstances of the individual foundation.

It is not always feasible or even socially advantageous to adopt the abstract ideal in investment diversification. The Duke Endowment, as an extreme example of prohibited diversification, is limited in its investments to a narrow list of securities by its indenture of trust. Severe donor-imposed restrictions on investments govern a relatively small number of other large foundations, a number not likely to increase materially if only for the reason that men of great wealth and their counsel now are alert to the consequent dangers. Obstruction of diversification now is less formal and rigid and is commonly less durable. Should a donor today intend a recipient foundation to hold a block of stock for a relatively long period, he may be confident that the trustees will respect his wishes as far as legally permitted without a formal mandate. After all, he selected them, usually serves on the board himself, and can trust that even after his death his wishes and those of his surviving family will be influential.

Trustees face a psychologically difficult choice when it is clear that a foundation would gain in money or public confidence by disposing of all or a large portion of donated securities with a by-product of disadvantage to the donor or his heirs. They are, nevertheless, under fiduciary responsibility to do so. No private interest remains in funds dedicated to public benefit by donation to a foundation. However, it should not be inferred that securities in a business dominated by the donor or his family should be precipitiously liquidated. It frequently is more advantageous to hold blocks of donated securities in a family controlled corporation. Trustees with respect for fiduciary principles can do so without showing favoritism to the donor or his family. Trustees of smaller foundations may find themselves with concentrated holdings for which there is no real or ready market despite a good income return. It also may be difficult to dispose of large blocks of stock in a giant corporation without distressing financial sacrifice. The Ford Foundation, funded with an enormous block of Ford Motor Company shares, probably was not surprised that it lost heavily by disposing of a large percentage of donated shares; nevertheless, it deliberately made the sacrifice in the interest of diversification and out of regard for public sentiment. The common and obvious creation of foundations as a device for avoidance of gift and inheritance taxes so large that they could only be paid by sale of a control-threatening interest in a closely held corporation has aroused such strong opposition that diversification within some reasonable period is wise and inevitably will become the rule.

A proposed rule that no tax deduction should be allowed a donor of a controlling interest in a corporation if he or his family control the recipient foundation would be difficult to enforce and costly in philanthropic terms. Control of a corporation may require ownership or control of only a relatively small percentage of voting stock. Control of a foundation does not require membership of the donor or a member of his family on the board of trustees, only of persons beholden to him or merely good friends. Effective legislative or administrative definition of corporation or foundation control is a practical impossibility. The philanthropic cost of enforced immediate diversification of investments by sale of any major holding in a donor-related corporation or the legal discouragement of trusteeship by the donor or a member of his family would discourage the creation of new foundations. One may ask if such foundations as the W. K. Kellogg Foundation, the Julius Rosenwald Fund, the Lilly Endowment, The Duke Endowment, and many others that have been of great public benefit would have been established if the proposed restrictions had been in effect. Strict enforcement of proper fiduciary behavior together with diversification over a reasonable number of years, possibly something in the order of 25 years, would be enough to prevent the development of economic dynasties based

on the tax exemption of philanthropic funds and reduce the risk
of financial loss to charity through failure of a single corporation.
It also would provide protection against the possible necessity
for selling securities on an inadequate market, always a problem
in disposing of small, specialized business or large blocks of
securities under pressure. It is in point that several large foundations presently diversifying as a matter of voluntary policy not
only are selling at carefully selected intervals, but also are ex-
changing securities with other entirely unrelated foundations and
making grant payments in securities in place of cash in order
not to run the risk of depressing the market.

Foundations managed by trustees with the highest ideals of
business ethics and law observance can slip into gray areas of
activities resulting in personal gain for donors and trustees without the slightest ulterior purpose, without adverse effect on program, and without incurring serious criticism. Incidental self-
serving that does not affect finances or program, as by depositing
funds in a bank with which a trustee is associated or employing
close business associates or friends as counsel or in other capac-
ities, may not be thought of as self-serving or, if so, is usually
condoned, although sometimes subject to mild questioning by
the punctilious. Possibly such incidental favoritism is excused
in recognition of the fact that the selection of counsel, employees,
banks, and investment houses, as also the selection of trustees
previously mentioned, is commonly and possibly best made on
the basis of intimate personal knowledge and the extra incentive
for good service because of a natural desire for continued good
personal and business relations.

How sensitive should trustees be about gains through routine
foundation transactions with business associates and friends or
with a corporation in which they have a substantial interest or
by which they are employed, but do not control? That there is
a difference of opinion about the good taste, if not the ethics, in [1]
such matters is illustrated by the refusal of some foundation
trustees and treasurers to accept foundation accounts in banks
of which they are officers or directors, in contrast with most who
are without qualms and meet no objections in doing so. In further
illustration of how fine the line may be, there is the case of a
foundation trustee and finance committee member who showed

no hesitation about the brokerage fees on security purchases by the foundation received by the investment company in which he was a partner, but did not allow the company to take the normal extra profit on the purchase of a new stock offered by a syndicate of which it was a member. Not all mildly questionable foundation financial transactions can be enjoined, but it would be praiseworthy if the rule were alertly followed that when there is the slightest doubt about ethics or good taste in any contemplated transaction, "Don't do it."

Propriety in Foundation Programs

Incongruity between foundation concern with human welfare and the nature of a business in which investment may be made is a gray area easily and frequently overlooked. At the general level, there are many who question the propriety of investment in an alcoholic beverage business, a race track or hotel with gambling facilities, cigarette companies or delapidated housing, but there are others who see nothing wrong with such sources of philanthropic income. More specifically, should a foundation concerned with health invest in a tobacco company? Does an economic welfare program seem compatible with the purchase of securities of a corporation with questionable labor policies? Does activity in the field of civil rights require an investment policy restricting purchases to businesses that have positive programs for the employment and service of Negroes and others handicappped by discrimination? Indeed, should not any foundation be mindful in its investments of the social utility of a company's product and the social standards of its practices? The source of funds may or may not have an influence on a foundation's activities, but it is natural for the public to think that they do. More basic is the principle that funds dedicated to public benefit should not draw their income from discordant enterprises.

Money isn't everything. The worth of the services of foundation trustees depends more on the programs they develop and support than on their management of finances. Although no Congressional investigative body or private evaluation of foundations has failed to recognize their substantial positive role in American life, all, including those most favorably inclined, also have challenged some consequences of the freedom of foundation choice of objective and manner of operation presently encouraged by law and public sentiment. The multitude of possible program choices and the corresponding criticisms may be viewed from a variety of points of vantage. Here the major disputed choices will be grouped, somewhat arbitrarily, first, as related to good judgment and integrity in the selection and operation of programs; second, as questions involving disputed ideological orientations; and, third, as belief in, or doubts about, the current utility of foundations as instruments for the advancement of human welfare.

Choice of Program.   There is no yardstick by which any one of the general areas of philanthropic endeavor allowed a foundation by the Internal Revenue Code may be measured to establish its importance in relation to any other area. Within each area, however, there are practically infinite choices of smaller sub-areas and specific activities from which selections must be made. It is at the point of these sub-choices that good judgment becomes crucial, where detailed information and knowledgeable advice is essential, and the quality of judgment may be rationally disputed. This is why previous emphasis was given to the need for experienced trustees, consultants, and staff.

Assuming that the wisest possible program choices have been made, there still remain many detailed questions of management policy that, if neglected or dubiously decided, are subject to adverse comment or condemnation. Excessive delay in getting a program under way or in acting on specific proposals is not unusual. Secrecy in defense of the right of privacy of an applicant, as has been said, is an obligation, but raises suspicion of favoritism, prejudice, and ideological bias if carried much beyond that point. Undue reticence concerning policy and positive actions suggests avoidance of the full accounting expected of a public trust. Pressure on a recipient, however subtle or unintended, to adapt to foundation orientation and interests, with a consequent weakening of recipient autonomy, needs to be avoided. Foundations stressing innovation properly are more interested in fresh approaches than in ongoing activities of established worth and also are inclined to limit support to "seed money" for just a few initiating years. Both policies are bitterly attacked by many whose needs do not fit the innovative pattern as "gimmickitis" and "hit and run" tactics.[35]

Earlier in this essay it was argued that foundations should cooperate with each other more frequently than they do, but it is not good judgment to pass around negative reactions to an agency, individual, or field of activity. It is equally unwise for an officer or trustee of one foundation to be overly persuasive in urging that another foundation support a favored institution, as often is done, sometimes with implicit suggestion of later reciprocity, although, of course, there is no objection to reasonable effort at persuasion if the proposal is within the other foundation's program. A bane of foundation officers is the meeting, usually with a good lunch or dinner, called by a foundation, at which the case of a needy agency is hawked with "hard sell" techniques. Such sales efforts are in bad taste, offer a basis for decision far inferior to the normal direct application foundation by foundation, and should be avoided. Furthermore, they can be cited in support of the unjustified allegation that there are foundation "interlocks," informal cabals, exercising undue influence on the social order.

Alertness is required concerning the distinction between education, especially civic education, and propaganda, for it sometimes is slight and only in the eye of the beholder. One man's concept of education is, indeed, commonly another man's propaganda. If a foundation activity can be interpreted as a direct attempt to influence legislation, tax exemption can be lost, provided that it is a substantial element in the foundation's program. Nevertheless, if the result of a foundation activity definitely has relevance to a legislative question, there need be no reticence about offering testimony in writing or in person on invitation from the government. In such a circumstance, the presentation of data and opinion bearing directly on legislation is not legally prohibited and is a foundation obligation.

Occasionally a foundation is offered money by other than the basic donor. If offered openly by a private individual, a corpora-

---

[35] For a rejoinder to these criticisms, see Warren Weaver, letter published in *Science*, vol. 138, December 1, 1967, pp. 1133–1134.

tion, the government, or another foundation and for use within the foundation's competence and proper program, there is no reason that it should not be accepted. Russell Sage Foundation, for example, has happily accepted a small legacy, several relatively large sums from other foundations, and a number of government research grants. This is in accord with the basic idea that has resulted in the establishment of over 200 community foundations designed to accept gifts and legacies of any size for more efficient philanthropic expenditure under appropriate unified management. Such offers, however, need careful scrutiny to make certain that the purpose, if specified, is proper both ethically and in terms of the foundation's program and performance ability, and also not merely a questionable tax dodge. The justified furor aroused by the disclosure that the Central Intelligence Agency had used foundations as a secret conduit for the support of activities definitely not philanthropic in nature stands as a warning against covert use of foundations as tools for ulterior purposes, but should not be regarded as discouraging cooperation with a government agency in normal, aboveboard projects.

All the foregoing cautions add up to nothing more than the common sense need for efficiency and probity, which are the only answers to irresponsible allegations that any more than a very small proportion of foundations have been guilty of poor judgment and duplicity in program development and operation. There are some outright bad foundations that should be severely penalized or terminated, some misguided and ineffective ones that need stimulation to improvement, and some that have been excellent on the whole but have made a number of errors in judgment. In short, foundations are not unlike industries, retail stores, or banks in their management, but with the distinction that their benevolent character raises public expectations to an unattainable but coveted target near perfection.

Ideology and Values.   No matter how carefully and wisely foundations choose their areas of activity and their specific projects, there is bound to be criticism unless minimized by faint-hearted restriction of allocations to the socially orthodox agencies previously referred to as "blue chip" institutions. This is an inevitable circumstance in a democracy that takes pride in individualism and encourages diversity of opinion. Three main ideological themes are evident in controversies about the social orientation of foundation programs. The questions in dispute are whether or not foundation programs are a powerful force for, first, maintaining a status quo favoring an advantaged and wealthy "establishment"; second, a contrary force for economic and social change in sympathy with radical, left-wing ideologies; or, third, a somewhat randomly unsettling influence on the "American way of life" because of innovating research and experimental projects intended to find new ways of resolving social problems.

Foundations do permit continuing concentrations of wealth in the control of self-perpetuating boards of trustees assumed to be biased in favor of the existing social order for the reason that they have been successful in it. Foundations, as any business corporation, medical facility, university, or other powerful organization, can be sources of power misused for anachronistic obstruction of social change. For example, in a controversy between labor and industrial owners, it is possible and it seems probable that stock held by foundations would be voted for the owners' position. It also is assumed that research and other projects would be selected in such a way that the results most likely would favor the wealthy rather than the daily worker. It was the assumption that foundations naturally would be conservative and support their business interests to the disadvantage of labor that led to their investigation by the United States Senate Industrial Relations Commission in the second decade of the present century and resulted in a majority report critical of their economic power. The fears of liberals concerned about foundations in the struggles of the underprivileged for improvement of their condition raised such strong objections to the request for a federal charter for The Rockefeller Foundation in 1910 that after a three-year delay a legislative charter was sought and obtained from New York State. Considerable liberal skepticism concerning foundation conservative influence continued until well after World War I and is still in evidence.

As might have been expected, individual foundations turned out over the years to be conservative, liberal, and something in between in their economic and social outlooks. Some have been

established with the obvious intention of the donor that their
funds would be used to support the status quo, or even the status
quo ante. None of any size has been created with a purpose truly
radical. The orientation of the vast majority is definitely philanthropic in the meaning of the word as applied to the support of
humanitarian, educational, scientific, or religious activities. The
outstanding large foundations, those that have worried the liberals most, have not been in the control of men foolish enough
to attempt to use them to stop the social clock, contrary to the
apparent assumption of the Walsh Commission majority. The
basic explanation of this seeming conflict with assumed personal
interests is simple. Outstandingly successful men in business and
the professions clearly of superior quality and integrity rarely
have made their marks by attempting to stem social or economic
tides. They are aware of the necessity for adaptive social change,
of the desirability of venturesome research and innovative practice, and know that the perfect society is a goal not yet reached.

It is this recognition by the trustees of influential foundations
of the need for ordered social change, which by now should have
allayed the fears of the liberals, that has alarmed conservatives of
the far right and bothered the less extreme and less sophisticated
defenders of the status quo. The extremists have supported their
fears by interpreting pioneering research and innovative projects
as socially subversive, if not communistic. The more rational
conservatives have largely avoided such nonsensical extrapola-
tion and have been more concerned about foundation interest in
finding new ways to social betterment challenging to widespread
beliefs. They also have worried about the few inadvertent grants
made to agencies or individuals later found or alleged to have had
far-left beliefs or radical leanings or associations.

This latter concern of the temperate conservatives deserves a
considered response, perhaps best offered in the final report of
the Cox Committee. This report, completed after the death of
Representative Cox, was signed by the six surviving members of
the Committee, although one member, Representative Reece,
added the parenthetical reservation following his signature that
the Committee had had not enough time for the task with which
it was charged. There was agreement by the Committee that
"There can be no reasonable doubt concerning the efforts of the

Communist Party both to infiltrate the foundations and to make use, so far as it was possible, of foundation grants to finance Communist causes and Communist sympathizers." It then went on to say that "A few small foundations became the captives of the Communist Party. Here and there a foundation board included a Communist or a Communist sympathizer. Occasionally a Communist managed to secure a position on the staff of a foundation or a staff member was drawn into the Communist orbit. Our investigation, hurried by lack of time, indicates that very few actual Communists or Communist sympathizers obtained positions of influence in the foundations. However, there are some unhappy instances where the Committee is convinced infiltration occurred."[36] The same can be and has been said about a number of industries, government agencies, publishers, universities, and churches. For the sake of perspective, a reminder may be desirable that the report was prepared at a time of exceptional concern about subversion and when the terms "Communist" and "Communist sympathizer" were bandied about. Honest mistakes and susceptibility to double-dealing, as well as purposeful misconduct, are deplorable, but they do occur.

Influential foundation programs inevitably arouse controversy. Many seemingly "safe" grants can be the source of attack by those whose motto apparently is *semper idem*. Foundations concerned with research and the improvement of human conditions are intervening in social development, interfering with comfortable ways of life, and consequently disturbing those who like things as they are. As expected, foundations have been both praised and attacked for their influential role in improving the condition of the Negro American. But who would expect the attacks that have been made in Congress and elsewhere on undramatic projects concerned with juvenile delinquency or troop

---

[36] *Final Report of the Select Committee to Investigate Foundations and Other Organizations* (Washington: Government Printing Office, January 1, 1953), pp. 6–7. The later report to the following Congress by the Special Committee to Investigate Tax-Exempt Foundations and Comparable Organization came to no reliable conclusions. Its hearings ended midstream in a turmoil and a minority report signed by two of the five members of the committee sharply challenges that of the majority. One of the three members who signed the majority report made his signature practically meaningless by a footnote to it saying that he had not modified or altered the views he had expressed in the Cox Commission Report.

morale during World War II? Or broad deprecation of empirical study of social problems? Even the deservedly renowned work of The Rockefeller Foundation for the eradication of hookworm was derided as fostering a myth about the entry of the parasite through bare feet and as motivated by a Rockefeller desire to make and sell shoes. Russell Sage Foundation efforts to develop model legislation for the protection of the needy poor from loan sharks were challenged as recommending excessive legal rates of interest for small loans, oppressive to the poor, and affording unnecessary if not self-dealing advantage to favored private lenders. Even the support of nascent areas in the physical and biological sciences, such as atomic physics and molecular biology, is challenged as "gimmickitis" and detrimental to the relevant disciplines as a whole, to academic institutions and society, especially, but not exclusively, by those who are well established in more orthodox research. Anything new, of course, is upsetting and therefore economically, socially, or politically radical to some segment of the population.

Also unavoidable are actual undesirable consequences that may flow from grants judged without reservation to be of potential human benefit. The reduction of sickness and death rates, a benefit to which quite a number of foundations have made notable contributions, has contributed to rapid population increases in many countries without comparable increase in the supply of food. The foundation-financed cyclotron at the University of California, without the slightest such anticipation by the funding foundation, supplied the first uranium 235 for the atom bomb. Relief in cash or kind can weaken the recipient's self-respect and have a pauperizing effect. Study of social institutions and living patterns can reduce the socializing influence of cherished behavior standards. An effective specific for venereal disease or an acceptable and certain contraceptive may encourage deviant sexual behavior. An agriculturally valuable weed killer, a chemical of industrial worth, or a biological discovery of benefit in medical practice may be used as a brutal weapon of war. Psychological knowledge gained with foundation support has contributed much to educational practice and mental therapy, but it also has been used for shoddy salesmanship and brainwashing. Foundations must either avoid innovation or reconcile themselves to the fact that regrettable consequences may follow from prideful achievements. The balm when the risk is taken is in the practically universal agreement that progress always has its costs and that foundation benefits have far outweighed their social price.

A very large percentage of the grants of foundations of all types run very little risk of serious ideological opposition, but none is intrinsically immune. Shy or antagonistic renunciation of all opportunity to be venturesomely influential in human betterment by giving only supportive or gently developmental grants to popularly accepted agencies may be good protective practice. But no amount of caution will avoid all criticism. Even the most routine of grants of these kinds may be deemed contrary to public interest in consequence of clashing biases and interpretations. Harvard University is regarded by many as representative of the very best in higher education, and by others as an already too wealthy bastion of a self-centered establishment. During World War II the Red Cross was held to be practically a mother substitute, but also was castigated for its policy on the acceptance of Negro blood donations. Contributions to welfare agencies may be praised or criticized because of religious orientation or policy regarding birth control advice to clients. The donation of a playground for public use may be regarded as an invasion of private rights by neighbors who object to the anticipated noise or, if some obsolete housing needs to be razed, as a disaster by those dispossessed. Discouraging and galling as it is to be questioned concerning motivation and good judgment in benevolence, criticism of grants firmly believed to be orthodoxly beneficial is the easiest to take. There may be comfort in the thought that if there is no criticism at all, probably nothing worth mentioning has been accomplished.

The Social Utility of Foundations.   More discouraging and exasperating than either of the ill-founded charges of excessive conservatism or radical influence is the view that foundations have outlived, or are about to outlive, their usefulness. This view usually is patronizingly accompanied by credit for praiseworthy work in the past and recognition that to some extent foundations still serve some purposes that are worthy, but perhaps not crucial. All in all, it is said by those who take this position, the possible and occasional actual misuses of foundations can and should be avoided by severe limitation of the creation of new foundations and their elimination over time, now that the government has accepted responsibility for all fields of foundation activity except religion, one that can be and largely is taken care of by private donations. Indeed, the argument continues, direct personal donations can and may better serve philanthropic ends than foundations which are mainly conduits of convenience to the donor.

The donor convenience of foundations offhand may seem of slight importance in philanthropy in comparison with the tax exemption still available for direct benefactions if foundations did not exist. The obvious reply is that such convenience violates no ethical principle and unquestionably has stimulated the flow of private funds into works for public benefit. If such funds are desired by the public—existing legislation is evidence that this is the case—the convenience of the foundation as a philanthropic mechanism hardly may be denied those who have established family foundations, particularly the relatively smaller ones, or may wish to do so in the future. Convenience, however, is only of secondary consideration in evaluation of the larger, long-lived and efficiently operated foundations. The advantage of these foundations to society is outstanding and lies in their rational organization and philanthropic experience and expertise. They have become institutions with practical efficiency beyond that to be expected of a direct donor, likely to be most knowledgeable in the field where he made his money or in the manner he conserved his inheritance. Over the years, there is a strong tendency—almost a certainty—for foundations of great size to become institutionalized, particularly after the donor and his heirs no longer are involved. The kind of rational allocation of funds the great foundations practically alone can provide contradicts the argument that direct giving is all that is desirable. With regard to the claim that the government now is willing and able to take care of the health, welfare, educational, and research needs now served by foundations, this may be conceded only if it is believed that there are or soon will be no lacunae in the relevant government programs, that there are no areas in these fields which the government will avoid for political reasons, and that there is no value for comparative purposes in humanitarian activities free of governmental control.

Trustees' responsibilities are not limited merely to compliance with the legal requirements of fiduciaries and the conduct of a program in accordance with the letter of the donor's mandate. Their obligations include constant challenging awareness that their personal values and their judgments concerning the best interests of society will and should guide their interpretation of the donor's purpose and their actions as trustees. At the same time, they need also to be aware that whatever their valued beliefs, there are others who hold contrary views with equal sincerity, views that in a pluralistic and changing society may need to be incorporated in their own thinking. Continuing alertness is required to the possibility that a change in program, in manner of operation and even, although rarely, in the mandate itself may be desirable.

The contrast between present industrialization, population growth, and urban concentration in the United States and the earlier more agricultural and rural conditions prevailing in the period of foundation development has created serious problems of adaptation to current needs and social values. Thought must be given by both trustees and makers of public policy to the degree of relevance of traditional charitable ideals and practices to the social needs and other practical considerations in philanthropy as they exist in the United States today.

Charity, a synonym for philanthropy currently in disfavor as patronizing and an affront to beneficiaries, was praiseworthy in the lands that contributed most to the development of American civilization. Judeo-Christian teachings, coming by way of Rome, formed the basis of English law and practice, which in turn have been basic in American philanthropy from colonial times to the present. Each country made its modifications and contributions to the stream of borrowing. The factual and legal history of charity along the way to the present, especially in the Elizabethan period in England, offers perspective and is well worth review. What is most relevant for present purposes, however, is the fact that some criteria by which foundations frequently are judged as praiseworthy, or the reverse, are the product of this history inadequately modified to meet the needs of a changing order.

Traditionally, philanthropic aid should be a matter of personal involvement rather than a remote service to the needy. It is expected to meet an existing personal need directly and without delay and be promptly ameliorative rather than preventive in purpose. Both the beneficiaries and the form of benefaction long have been commonly regarded as matters for the donor to decide, with no professional intermediary required. Charitable donations still are thought of as private gifts, preferably with no publicity and with no expectation until recently that the public would share the cost through tax exemption or require other than possibly religious accountability. These attitudes and standards prevail today in fact and in law insofar as aid is given to family members, friends, and beggars, certainly a large if quantitatively unknown fraction of American philanthropic giving. A large and also unknown fraction of the American population is critical of foundation giving that does not meet these traditional tests.

Only a relatively small family foundation is likely to operate in accord with the traditional charitable precepts, nor is it easy for it to do so in the larger urban concentrations. Not only, as has been said, is it difficult today for a donor to obtain direct and adequate knowledge of recipient individuals and agencies, or to acquire an adequate understanding of social needs, but also the persuasiveness and pressure of professionalized agencies frequently is practically irresistible. It may be that foundations have grown so greatly in number in recent years, at least in part, because philanthropy no longer can depend on the personal experience and wisdom of the donor. Social institutions do seem to have a habit of developing in response to social needs somewhat in advance of the views of contented population elements. Although it is common to note various lags in social adjustment, there are also instances of leads in social action that are ahead of the recognition of new situations on the part of most of the general public. As philanthropy as a whole is responding to social change, so foundations must be prepared to respond to changes in social needs and newer knowledge of ways of meeting them.

It is said that the safest way to predict the weather is to assume that on any one day it will be about the same as the day before. The same assumption of persistence may be used to predict a foundation's policies, program, and grants from year to year, decade to decade, and even longer, with little regard for changing relevant circumstances that also are not subject to prediction on any other assumption. Consequently there is a good chance that a foundation may find itself contending with yesterday's problems. Of course, yesterday's problems may be expected to continue as tomorrow's problems, but there also may be new problems in no less need of attention. The character of foundation opportunities shifts from time to time, sometimes with unanticipated rapidity, and can easily be overlooked for quite a while.

In an imaginative yet realistic paper concerned with the future of foundations, Alan Pifer has asked who in 1936 could have foreseen the major events between that year and 1968 that have materially modified the social order throughout the world.

> In that span of years we have witnessed the coming of the second World War; the founding of the United Nations; the Cold War; the advent of Communism in China; the end of colonialism; the revolution of men of color in Asia, Africa, and the United States; nuclear bombs; the space race; urbanization, and the decline of our great cities; unprecedented economic growth in the industrialized nations; the fantastic expansion of higher education in the United States; and the centrality of television, air travel, and the computer. All of these developments could almost certainly have been foreseen by someone 32 years ago. But their relationships to each other, their configuration in forming the immensely complex world of 1968 would, I believe, have defied even the greatest minds of that day.[37]

Such unanticipated events can and have required fundamental shifts in foundation programs and even in donors mandates.

Basic change in foundation mandate requires court action, whether or not the donor is still alive and desires one made. As explained in the preceding essay by Wilbert Moore, court action may be initiated under the *cy pres* doctrine when a mandated purpose has become impossible or impractical (perhaps because a suitable agency or class of persons a donor wished to aid no longer can be found), contrary to law, or the available funds have turned out to be too limited for the original stated purpose. The *cy pres* doctrine is not accepted in all jurisdictions in the United

---

[37] Alan Pifer, *The Foundation in the Year 2000* (New York: The Foundation Library Center, 1968), p. 6.

States. The very similar doctrine of deviation permitting departures from mandates (generally in administrative requirements) at times has been stretched to allow changes in purpose. There are some who believe it should be expanded to take the place of *cy pres* in those jurisdictions where *cy pres* is not accepted. American courts have been relatively strict in acting on petitions under either doctrine, both in judging the necessity for change and in deciding on whether or not the proposed new purpose is as close as it should be to the donor's first intent, but there is evidence of a liberalizing tendency. Resort to such appeals mostly has been by trusts, usually comparatively small ones, rather than by corporate foundations. In recent decades when most grant-making philanthropic funds have been established, detailed specification of beneficiaries and fields generally has been avoided. "Tracking the statute," that is, listing all or nearly all the philanthropic objectives approved by statute for tax exemptions, eliminates the likelihood that resort to court action for desired modification in objective will be necessary. As has been suggested, there are those who regret omnibus charters that reveal nothing about donors' specific intentions, but they do have merit in view of the fact that neither the *cy pres* nor the deviation doctrines meet the problems of program adjustment consequent to social change if a foundation is severely limited in stated purpose. An original purpose may still be possible, and worthy, and thus not truly subject to *cy pres* action, and still be rather outmoded relative to more important needs not foreseen by the donor. A restriction on types of investment or on the character of organization may not warrant a court-approved deviation, and still prevent trustees and staff from making otherwise sensible changes.

Foundations with broad purpose charters or instruments of trust obviously are limited in their actual benefactions by the size of their funds and the preferences of their trustees. Funds may grow or diminish. Preferences may change for personal reasons, in accord with the predilections of new trustees, or merely insensibly with time. Ideally the purposes and operating practices of foundations are best continued or altered by conscious and informed choice. This requires periodic reconsideration of program and administration, preferably involving the aid of others than the members of the board and staff. The advice of outsiders is desirable not only for objectivity, but also to bring to bear divergent views and relevant expertise not available within the foundation. There may be times when such reconsideration best may be done on the basis of a review of activities and alternative opportunities prepared independently by outsiders, possibly by a management consultant organization, an individual, or an ad hoc group. An independent program audit, however, has the disadvantages of discontinuity in approach and dilution of the possible educational contribution to trustees and staff which can be gained by an internally directed review. Involvement in a review directed by trustees and staff, if available, increases philanthropic sophistication of lay management, identifies trustees and staff with findings, and reduces resistance to the possible conclusion that drastic change is in order. It may be necessary gently to retire some trustees and staff members. Those who continue require reorientation most readily begun by active participation in the procedures resulting in program revision.

If on review and reconsideration of activities the decision is made to embark on a new program, primary attention needs to be given to the orderly termination of the abandoned program. Inadvertent damage otherwise may be done. Particular care must be taken that previous beneficiaries, especially those that have received support over a number of years and may have come, with or without adequate reason, to rely on its continuation, be given time to adjust to their new financial situation. As the present writer has said in an earlier publication,

> Abrupt termination of activities in a particular field is rarely if ever justified, except perhaps in cases of dismal failure, and even then human considerations may not be ignored with good conscience. Provision for a period of readjustment ordinarily should be made for agencies and individuals that have become heavily dependent on a foundation which then deserts their field of work. Time is needed for the search for other sources of support. And if this proves unavailing, arrangements should be made for decent burial.
>
> Giving advice and help in finding other sources of support is humane and proper, as is also assistance to individuals in finding new employment, should this turn out to be necessary. It is satisfying to be able to record the fact that such evidences of concern for those involved in terminated programs are quite common in the history of the older, better known foundations,

and possibly is the case of others about which less information is readily available. Indifference under the circumstances is inexcusable.[38]

Agencies that have received but a single grant, possibly for a specific operation to be completed within a given time and with no reasonable implication of renewal, present no problem. Presumably the deserted field in general also requires no further attention, on the assumption that it would not have been abandoned if regarded as both worthy and in financial distress. It is the needy individual and agency that have come to rely upon a foundation's aid, whether or not based on any justified implication drawn from previous relations with the foundation, that require some softening of the blow in the form of a reasonably generous terminal grant and advice if requested.

Publicizing Foundation Activities

Any change in foundation interest and manner of operation magnifies the benefits to be obtained by full reporting of program objectives and activities to the public in general and particularly to the newly eligible potential applicants. It is no less imperative that past clientele promptly be informed that future applications in their field will fail of consideration as a matter of foundation policy regardless of apparent merit. Here the word "clientele" is used to include not only those who actually have received grants, but also the wider range of formerly potential applicants. There will be a material reduction in unhappy correspondence and somewhat embarrassing interviews if program changes are carefully explained in a widely distributed printed report, perhaps the first annual report after the change is adopted but also possibly in a special brochure for added emphasis. Common courtesy, of course, requires that those persons and agencies that have had grants over a period of years and may expect more to be told in a more personal manner by correspondence or by visit that their future ineligibility is a result of policy and not of dissatisfaction

---

[38] Donald R. Young, "Changes in Field of Activity," in Henry Sellin, editor, *Proceedings of the Third Biennial Conference on Charitable Foundations*, New York University (Albany, N.Y.: Matthew Bender & Co., Inc., 1957), p. 51.

with their standard of performance in the discontinued area of interest.

An annual, or perhaps biennial, public report covering objectives, new grants and those still active, and investments, receipts, and expenditures is a foundation obligation even in the absence of any modification in policy. It is, however, an obligation that is only slowly now coming to be accepted by even the larger of the newer foundations. Failure to issue such reports has a number of possible explanations, such as the fear of a deluge of applications, the time-consuming nuisance of preparation, the belief that benefactions are a private matter, and the possible embarrassment of public disclosure of a seemingly helter-skelter list of grants. Whatever the explanation, none can outweigh the principle that there is an obligation to account to the public for the stewardship of a public trust.

It can be and is argued that the report to the federal government on Treasury Department Form 990-A, required of most foundations properly speaking, is an adequate accounting of stewardship. (Note that of the various organizations exempt from income tax under Section 501(c)(3) of the Internal Revenue Code, religious organizations, educational organizations that have an organized faculty and regular body of pupils or students, and charitable organizations wholly or predominantly dependent upon government funds or upon current contributions from the general public are not required to make an accounting on Form 990-A.) It is further claimed that the states have responsibility for overseeing foundation stewardship and do so in those where a large proportion are located, as in New York, California, Massachusetts, and Illinois. There is no need here to debate the effectiveness with which the federal government and the several states exercise their supervisory powers other than to say that it varies from near zero to something still far short of perfection. Foundations vary so much in the provisions of their charters and instruments of trust and in their operations that no simple reporting form is suitable for all. Furthermore, basic government reporting practices have been developed for profit-making organizations and with financial and tax questions in mind. This has not made adaptation for foundation reporting a simple matter. Formal reports to the government consequently are difficult for foundations to make on the forms supplied and are not revealing of much more than financial status and transactions. Insofar as they are available to the public they do not tell much about the performance of the stewards in service to the public. They are difficult of access and interpretation for the ordinary citizen. Form 990-A does have value for the experienced fund-raiser and has been made reasonably accessible by the deposit of copies of the public part in The Foundation Center in New York City and in its regional depositories.

No doubt the reticence of foundations about full public reporting is in some measure the consequence of failure to appreciate that it can serve as more than an accounting of stewardship. Reference previously has been made to opportunities for interfoundation cooperation. Published foundation reports obviously are one simple way of inter-foundation communication by which common interests may readily become known and lead either to joint effort where desired or avoidance of unnecessary and wasteful duplication. Most important of all, a published report if widely yet selectively distributed is the surest means for informing potential clientele of the nature of applications that will be considered on their merits and at the same time warning against those that will not be considered because of program limitations. Recalling that foundations do not just give money away, but are purchasing something with every allocation, the annual report needs to be written so that it will attract the best proposals from the best people and agencies in the chosen area of activity. Prepared with this dominant purpose, it still serves as a public accounting but its preparation is less of a dull chore of only historical import.

A periodic report is not the only form of public reporting that may be found useful by a foundation, particularly by the larger ones. Several issue brief printed reports between annual reports in which an account may be given of the findings of some completed project, a field of interest may be discussed, and new grants may be listed. Pamphlets outlining a field of activity have been distributed in order that potential applicants and others may be well informed about a foundation program, particularly a new one. The Ford Foundation, for example, in addition to its regularly published annual report, has issued numerous informative pamphlets concerning areas of special interest to it, as on its programs in law, administration of justice, and law enforcement, on international legal studies, on its grants in the field of population, on agricultural assistance in Asia, Africa, and Latin America, on the improvement of knowledge and practice of government, on the development of skills in foreign languages and English, and others. Articles in professional journals, news releases, and books telling about foundation programs and projects are not unusual. After an appreciable number of years of operation some foundations have arranged for histories of their work to be prepared and published. These histories have value as a record of experience if allowance is made for glossing over the less successful ventures and for bragging, but generally do not serve any forward-looking purpose. Conferences of leaders in an area of activity have been supported to discuss the nature and needs of areas of interest for the advantage of mutual understanding of the foundation and potential clients, sometimes resulting in valuable mimeographed or printed reports. The basic instrument for making known a foundation's program and activities, however, is the periodic report.

Small family foundations may think that their size and the fact that their grants really are matters of personal choice make anything more than the filling out of Form 990-A superfluous. This is at least debatable for many. It may be superfluous for those that will not even consider an unsolicited application or even acknowledge its receipt. It does seem reasonable to expect some response to an application, if only a printed explanatory declination on a postal card, in view of the tax exemption granted on the declaration that a public trust has been created. Many small foundations cannot consider new unsolicited applications because they have in effect, if not deliberately, decided on a continuing list of beneficiaries which leaves no surplus for allocation. For them a published annual report would serve no constructive purpose, but an account of the work supported over some period of years, perhaps five or even more, would be useful in its reassurance that the public was well served and also as a matter of historical record. The more flexible family foundation can benefit by periodic published statements of its interests and activities both by discouragement of "out of program" requests

and hopefully by stimulating at least an occasional attractive inquiry. Word will get around about the small and most reticent
foundation even in the absence of any formal public statement
and will be lamentably garbled and unnecessarily critical if allowed to depend solely on grapevine communication. The common belief and charge that family foundations are increasing in
number as rapidly as they are because of financial advantages to
donors unaccompanied by compensating gains for society may
only be answered by fully and freely telling the public what it is
gaining in exchange for tax exemption.

Informing the public about the social value of a foundation's
grants requires circumspect reporting. No foundation may take
more than fractional credit for the achievements of those to whom
it gave financial assistance. Even in the case of those projects
conducted directly by foundations the credit must be divided with
the many persons and institutions that contributed to the underlying ideas, facts, and techniques, and to the development of
operating personnel in addition to the people who did the work.
A foundation can report with appropriate pride that it made a
grant to some person or agency in support of what turned out to
be a major achievement, but the achievement was not the foundation's, nor was the grant more than one item, albeit possibly a
crucial one, in a long process of development. The maximum
gracious claim is that a contribution was made to a venture. The
nature of the venture, of course, should be described so that the
reason for supporting it is plain. Credit for the exercise of care
and good judgment in project selection is credit enough to justify
the privileges granted foundations and to give ample satisfaction
in a task well done to the donor, trustees, and staff.

The possibility is alleged that full public reporting of a foundation's policies and activities may become an unintentional influence for conservatism in the selection of fields and projects.
As has been said, the great majority of grants by even the most
innovative foundations quite properly involve little risk of serious
failure or strong popular criticism. Nevertheless, willingness to
support a relatively few projects that are truly venturesome in
objective or risky in operational prospects has been a praiseworthy trait of a significant number of foundations which needs
to be preserved and extended. It is a real question whether trustee

and staff awareness that a public accounting will be made may not unwittingly serve as a brake on entry into controversial fields, discourage support of projects that are not practically certain of success, and cause hesitation about financing the work of an individual who has not yet won his spurs or who may be regarded by some as a bit unorthodox in his professional work or private beliefs and behavior. This is a possibility against which foundation management needs to be on guard. It is, however, far outweighed by the positive contributions of public reporting to public understanding and appreciation of foundations as philanthropic instruments, to accurate knowledge of the reporting foundation's interests and program on the part of those from whom its clientele is drawn, and as a stimulus to active self-concern that activities are well considered.

If a periodic report is to make sense and not appear as a haphazard listing of random gifts, everyone involved in its preparation is compelled to ponder why each grant was made, to formulate a rational exposition of the principles that governed project selection individually and as a whole. This is not an easy task. Too often such search for principles will reveal that even if discoverable they were less influential than adventitious factors such as personal friendship, social or business pressure, or the pleasure of getting on a popular bandwagon. Often where governing principles are clear there will be projects that do not fit into the picture because they were selected as offering such exceptional opportunities that the limitations of a formal program should be violated. There is no good argument against this kind of departure from program, but it should be done deliberately and reported as such with the reason for the exception. It may well be that the absence of a defensible rationale is significantly related to the aversion of many foundations to public reporting. Interestingly enough, the foundations that have long issued periodic reports do offer their reasons for the choices they have made and are prepared to make on new applications.

The Measure of a Foundation

The performance of the trustees is the ultimate measure of a foundation's worth. This is fundamental, no matter what the extent of dependence by trustees in their decisions on information and advice of others or their delegation of operations to staff. Indeed, their wisdom, or lack of it, in the utilization of consultants and the selection of staff to supplement their own knowledge and experience is the best indicator of their performance. The effective discharge of their duties requires the determination of policy and its implementation either directly by their own actions or by surrogate. In either case there is no escape from responsibility.

Judgment of performance is made difficult by the fact that there is no single standard applicable to all foundations. Their entirely proper and socially desirable diversity does not permit any test comparable to the production or profit record of a business corporation or even to the comparative accomplishments of educational institutions or operating charitable agencies. As has been indicated earlier, their charters and instruments of trust vary greatly in objectives and in limits on operational freedom. Financial policy must vary in accord with restrictions possibly imposed by the donor and by state legislation and rulings, and with trustee judgment of financial needs for present or future philanthropic opportunities. Staff of varying skills and number may or may not be advantageous, depending on size and program. Major modifications in program may or may not be permitted or desirable. The frequency, extent, and form of public reporting in supplementation of Form 990-A differ with objectives and size. The common denominator of all foundations which are the subject of this essay is that they are tax-exempt legal entities for the management of private funds for public benefit, and nothing more. This is mainly why there is no formal association similar to those of various types of educational institutions and industries, why no code of good practice or ethics has been capable of formulation, why an informed public is needed as a moral force, and why dependence must be on federal and state government to prevent the abuse of tax exemption, foundation by foundation, and not, as in the case of academic institutions, primarily on self-policing.[39]

---

[39] For a discussion of divergent views concerning the possibility of and need for a code of foundation practice, see: Mortimer M. Caplin, "A Code of Practice Is Needed"; Donald R. Young, "A Foundation Code of Practice:

Yet there is one broad classification of foundations that has a practical value and should be recognized both by the public and by law. Most foundations, especially but not exclusively those more recently established and with the smaller endowments, for want of a better term may be designated as "proprietary" foundations. In this category are those foundations that essentially are instruments of personal convenience for the donor, his family, and possibly his heirs. Impersonal, institutionalized foundations constitute the second category. They are relatively few in number, but are mostly among the largest. Perhaps a third category should be recognized, those that have some characteristics of the two prime categories, mainly large foundations in transition from proprietary to institutional form, generally passing from a period of personal domination because of growing donor sophistication or after his death. They usually have endowments sufficiently large to attract the services of superior trustees.

Proprietary foundations offer the maximum possible tax exemption, permit the setting aside of funds when conveniently available for philanthropic purposes without immediate decision concerning ultimate disposal, and provide a businesslike mechanism for benevolence. Their grants do not differ significantly from those made by personal check. Essentially the same separate classification of such personal convenience foundations is recognized in their common designation as family foundations and tentatively has been recommended by Alan Pifer as deserving separate legal status.[40] It may be that "donor controlled" is an adequate name for them, but there has been difficulty in objectively defining "control" in such a way that it does not disadvantageously apply to some foundations that are not truly controlled by the donor or his family. The realistic distinction is not some proportion of family members on the board of trustees or what influence one or more of them may have on decisions, but whether or not the foundation serves as little or nothing more than a financial conduit. Family conduit foundations can and do serve

---

A Negative View"; and John W. Riehm, Jr., "More Is Needed Than a Code of Practice"; in Henry Sellin, editor, *Proceedings of the Seventh Biennial Conference on Charitable Foundations,* New York University (Albany, N.Y.: Matthew Bender & Co., Inc., 1965), pp. 237–267.

[40] Alan Pifer, previously cited, p. 9.

society as intended by the public and under the law. Their designation here as proprietary is by no means intended as a disparagement, but only to suggest that they should be recognized as what they are in fact.

If they were so recognized, it would be possible rationally to consider legislation allowing holdings up to absolute control in a family business, subject, of course, to safeguards against abuses of tax exemption and self-dealing. It would be in accord with the rule against private perpetuities if this were coupled with a requirement that all assets be disposed of by grants for purposes allowable for organizations with tax exemption under Section 501(c)(3) of the Internal Revenue Code within a specified time, either after a definite number of years or some period after the death of the donor. For reasons previously mentioned it seems wisest for long-term or perpetual foundations to diversify investments, yet an all-inclusive rule against concentration of holdings, particularly against control of a family business, would in the past probably have deterred the establishment of many outstanding foundations and no doubt would do so in the future. With income and endowment irrevocably dedicated to public benefit, active legal oversight to prevent chicanery, and relatively short life, the difference between direct individual or family ownership of a business and indirect control through a proprietary foundation is in favor of the public. Categorical distinction by law between proprietary and institutionalized foundations, long recognized by those experienced in the foundation field, would permit more appropriate and effective regulation of both types than is possible under present circumstances. Provision, of course, should be made for change from proprietary to institutionalized form if requested with satisfactory assurances of sincerity.

The measures of institutionalization are simple and obvious. Institutionalized foundations are not conduits for personal giving. They do not serve as a continuing convenience for the donor or anyone else. They may or may not have the donor or a descendant on the board of trustees, as do the Ford, Rockefeller, and Carnegie Foundations, but if so they serve possibly because of sentiment or personal interest in the foundation's program as any other trustee and without the slightest indication of belief that they have any peculiar claim on the way the money should be invested or spent. The policies and actions of institutionalized foundations are the result of independent and responsible trustee judgment. They keep the public, as well as the federal and relevant state governments, fully informed about what they have done and expect to do next. Community trusts, although established for multiple objectives by many individuals unrelated and most likely unknown to each other rather than by a single individual or family, are a prime example of institutionalized foundations. Company-sponsored foundations usually are proprietary in character. Undoubtedly it will be difficult to put the obviously existing distinctions between the two categories of foundations into legal language, but this is a pervasive characteristic of law rather than a unique and unsolvable limitation.

The measures of success or failure of proprietary foundations are measures of the proprietors rather than of the foundations as such. These foundations essentially are successful if they obey the letter and spirit of the law and fulfill their proprietors' needs. One may criticize the philanthropic judgment of a proprietor, but only on the same ground that one may differ with the personal gifts of an individual, as for contributing to an obsolescent, trivial, poorly managed, or socially dubious charitable, scientific, or educational institution while overlooking more significant philanthropic needs. Such criticism may be persuasively influential, but it does not justify interference so long as the requirements of tax exemption are met and public sentiment continues to regard benevolence as a private matter.

Institutionalized foundations, free of obligations to their donors and responsible only to the public, properly are subject to more stringent measures of worth. They are the property of the public by outright gift, although with the clear agreement that their funds will be managed by private trustees in pursuit of one or more specified objectives in accordance with a governmentally approved charter or instrument of trust. It is reasonable, even imperative, that such public monies be subject to investment policies and restrictions that are strictly in the public interest. It also is reasonable and imperative that expenditures be made on the basis of the best obtainable informed judgment, not merely on trustee personal predilections. In the abstract, private benevolence also should be based on something more than whim, but prevailing public sentiment to the contrary may not be disregarded. The endowments of institutionalized foundations, however, are not in fact, whatever the legal theory, the private property of the trustees. With the exception of possible donor trustees, they never were. The measure of success of institutionalized foundations is the wisdom with which expenditures are made in pursuit of objectives wisely selected.

Yet there remains the question of who is to judge what is a wise choice of field or project, and by what standard? Projects have a way of producing much less or more significant results than expected, of being much less or more controversial than anticipated. If misery loves company, as has been said, there may be comfort in remembering that this also is the way it is in business, industry, government, and family life. The perplexing problem is how to decide what is a foundation success or mistake. Only hindsight can approximate the answer to such a question, and then only with reservations because of social change, conflicting individual and group interests, and the inevitable possible use of discoveries and innovations for socially disadvantageous as well as beneficent ends. In a democratic, pluralistic, and changing society, the only manifest and ominous mistake of a law-abiding institutionalized foundation that can be readily observed in the making is the selection of incompetent trustees.

Index

Index